D0092881

Praise for

Much Ado About English

"*Ostrobogulously loquacious, linguistically ostentatious: a peregrination through pages of percurrent pleasure. A fun book and very rewarding to read.*"
Dr Michael Johnson, Open University

"*Help is at hand – whether your interest is neologisms or pleonasms. There are palindromic squares, no less, to test you, and even a run-down on how you can be really politically correct about that strange bloke lurking in the park – the sexually focused, cleanliness impaired, chronologically gifted individual, that is. Or to put it another way, that dirty old man.*"
Manchester Evening News

"*A tantalising taste of the massive range and downright bloody-mindedness of English, written in a lighthearted and engaging style.*"
Shropshire Magazine

Much Ado About English

Up and Down the Bizarre Byways

of a Fascinating Language

Richard Watson Todd

NICHOLAS BREALEY
PUBLISHING

LONDON · BOSTON

First published in the US by
Nicholas Brealey Publishing in 2007

First published in the UK in 2006
Reprinted 2007

3–5 Spafield Street   20 Park Plaza, Suite 1115A
Clerkenwell, London   Boston
EC1R 4QB, UK   MA 02116, USA
Tel: +44 (0)20 7239 0360   Tel: (888) BREALEY
Fax: +44 (0)20 7239 0370   Fax: (617) 523 3708
www.nicholasbrealey.com

ISBN-13: 978-1-85788-372-5
ISBN-10: 1-85788-372-1

British Library Cataloguing in Publication Data
A catalogue record for this book is available from the
British Library.

Library of Congress Cataloging-in-Publication Data

Todd, Richard Watson, 1966–
    Much ado about English : up and down the bizarre byways of a
fascinating language / Richard Watson Todd.
        p. cm.
    Includes index.
    ISBN-13: 978-1-85788-372-5
    ISBN-10: 1-85788-372-1
    1. English language--Etymology. 2. English language--Humor. 3.
English language--Usage. 4. Lexicology. 5. English language--History. I.
Title.

PE1574.T63 2007
422--dc22

                                                            2006015793

Printed in Finland by WS Bookwell.

Contents

Introduction

English is *the* international language, the most important language for science, commerce and entertainment. It's used in 115 countries, three times as many as the next language, French, and it dominates the internet with around 70 per cent of web pages in English. Chinese may have more native speakers than the 300–400 million people who speak English as a mother tongue, but this is more than made up for by the 200 million who speak English as a second language and the billion or so who are learning it.

English's dominance as a language is due to historical events – it is clearly not because English is more straightforward or logical than any of the other 6,000-odd languages in the world. Indeed, the complexity, unpredictability and sheer bloody-mindedness of much English usage make it one of the least suitable languages for its role. Why should a language that pronounces *colonel* as 'kernel' be so dominant? Or one that has over 20 ways of making a plural? Or one that contains such confusing pairs of words as *venal* and *venial*? Or one in which words shift meaning so often that several terms now mean the opposite to what they originally did? Or one in which a word like *dunce* is derived from the name of a genius? Or one that allows puns to be made in so many situations?

The surprises and curiosities in English don't end there. A word as modern-sounding as *earthling* actually dates back surprisingly far; relative nonentities such as a Cambridge innkeeper are immortalised in everyday phrases like *Hobson's choice*; and other obscure phrases such as *kick the bucket* are derived from the slaughterhouse. Simple, straightforward words like *die* and *queen* are replaced by oddities like *go the way of all flesh* and *baked bean*. Both birds and camels come in *flocks*; people repeat themselves in phrases like *bits and pieces* and *close proximity*; and accidentally swapping around the initial letters in a phrase such as *pack of lies* still results in an acceptable phrase – *lack of pies*. I could go on and on and on with such weird and wonderful examples, but the chapters in this book provide a depth of illustration and explanation way beyond what is possible in an introduction.

Obviously, it is not always possible to have definitive proof of any particular assertion in relation to a language that has been developing over thousands of years. This book does not attempt to be a textbook, but instead to stroll along the highways and byways of English through the ages.

English was obviously not selected for its role as a lingua franca because of any inherent simplicity or logic. Its massive range and variety of peculiarities, however, do make it a fascinating, absorbing and surprising language.

Part I

Origins

All our knowledge has its origins in our perceptions.

Leonardo da Vinci

E nglish has a long and venerable history stretching back well over 1,000 years. Even though it is called by the same name, the language of 1,000 years ago is not readily comprehensible today. The only constant about language is that it is changing. New words are continually being introduced, while older words die out or change their meanings. Some words, however, do stay the same.

This mixture of change and stasis makes the study of dates of first use and origins of words and of phrases or idioms a fascinating subject. The potential sources of new words are myriad. Some words are named after people, others are coined by respected authors with Shakespeare at the forefront, but marketing executives creating product names are also surprisingly influential. This first part looks at these issues of origins – where does the English we use today come from?

How old is an earthling?

The number of new words appearing in English is so great that several dictionary producers publish a whole supplement every year. Many of these inventions fade away quickly, but some stay around to become part of generally accepted English.

Sometimes we can guess the date at which the word was introduced into English quite accurately. For example, the title *Ms* (as opposed to Miss or Mrs) originates in the feminist movement following the Second World War. An educated guess might therefore put its first use in the 1960s. This is fairly close for its widespread adoption, although the title was first used in print in 1949.

Similarly, is it possible to make an educated guess about when the 1914–18 world war was first termed the *First World War*? Clearly, during the actual war itself people did not know that it would be the first of two major conflicts. Indeed, it was often referred to as the war to end all wars, and its official name was the Great War. It was only in 1931, when people came to accept that there was a real chance of another global conflict, that the 1914–18 war was sadly termed the First World War.

In trying to guess the original dates of **first use** of words, the nature of the word is important. Many of the oldest words in English are linked to agriculture and nature. Indeed, for many farm animals, such as *ewe*, *calf* and *ox*, for traditional agricultural implements, such as *plough* and *scythe*, and for common trees, such as *oak* and *elm*, it's impossible to give first dates as the words can be traced back with little change from Old English to Old German and beyond.

The dates of first use of other words are not as predictable. For example, we might associate *acid rain* with the growth of the environmental movement in the 1960s, but the phrase was first used in print in 1858. And perhaps we would anticipate *earthling* as dating to the first science-fiction novels at the turn of the twentieth century, but the word is first found in print in 1593 (albeit in the sense of a man of the earth). While we might expect *chairman* to date back as far as 1654, it is noteworthy that *chairwoman* follows relatively quickly in 1699 (especially given that it took until 1971 for political correctness to institute *chairperson*).

It's not only the dates of first use that can be surprising. The **origins** of words can also be unexpected. *Abet* derives from the Old French word *abeter*, meaning to bait or harass with dogs. This meaning later shifted to incite, which was then changed again to encourage and help. *Diaper* meaning nappy comes from the Old French for an ornamental cloth, *diaspre*, and the word can still be used for fabric with a distinctive pattern, although it wouldn't go down well in advertising. *Geek* is a variant of the Low German *geck*, meaning a fool, which in turn derives from the Scandinavian for to croak, the sound made by fools.

Place names can also have surprising origins. *Jeans* were originally made with a cotton cloth that was named after Jannes, the French word for Genoa in Italy where the cloth was produced; and the first *denim* came from Nîmes in France, so the fabric is 'de Nîmes'. *Laconic* refers to a person from the region of Lakonia or Sparta in ancient Greece, whose inhabitants were renowned for the brevity of their speech.

Can you guess which of the following suggested derivations is the correct one?

Condom (a preventive sexual sheath)
a   Dr Condom was a physician who lived during the reign
of King Charles II and gave his name to the condom.
b   Condom comes from the Italian *con* meaning with and
dometa meaning protection.
c   Condom is derived from the Italian for glove, guanto.

Jazz (a style of music)
a   As a lively musical style, jazz comes from the Creole
word *jass*, meaning strenuous sexual activity.
b   Jazz is a corruption of *chase*, indicating that the musicians constantly have to chase each other's notes in
playing jazz music.
c   Jazz is an abbreviation of *chastity music*, a term used
ironically to describe the style.

Pedigree (a line of ancestors)
a   The word pedigree was originally applied to people
rather than animals, and comes from the Latin *paedo*
for child plus *ad gratia*, meaning with favour.
b   A person's pedigree used to be shown in genealogical
trees. Someone decided that these patterns resembled
a crane's foot, and described them thus, using the
Middle French *pie de grue*.
c   Pedigree is a cross-linguistic combination of the
Scottish word *pet* for tamed animal and the French
phrase *à gré*, meaning favourable.

In fact, *condom* may be derived from the Italian word *guanto*;
jazz comes from the Creole word *jass*; and *pedigree* originates
in the Middle French term *pie de grue*.

Seemingly unconnected words can have a single origin. For instance, *angle* as a verb (meaning to fish), *angle* as a noun (meaning a corner) and *ankle* are all ultimately derived from the Proto-Indo-European word *ank*, meaning to bend (Proto-Indo-European was a language thought to have been spoken in southeastern Europe around 5,000 to 10,000 years ago). In the case of ankle, the derivation from Proto-Indo-European came through the Old English word *ancleow* to give its current meaning. The noun angle is derived from the Latin word for corner, *angulum*. For the verb angle, the Proto-Indo-European word for to bend became the root of the Old English word for fish hook, *angel*, which in turn led to the verb for to fish.

While there is a general consensus about the origins of the words above, for other words the derivation is a source of much controversy. A major bone of contention concerns *OK*, which has been adopted by more languages than any other word. First recorded in 1839, its suggested origins include that it:

- stands for oll korrect, a misspelling of all correct, often attributed to President Andrew Jackson.
- stands for Old Kinderhook, the nickname of President Martin van Buren.
- comes from the French Aux Cayes, a port in Haiti.
- is a corruption of the Choctaw word *okeh*, meaning it is so.
- comes from the initials of Obadiah Kelly, a shipping clerk responsible for initialling numerous bills of lading.
- stands for Orrin Kendall crackers, popular during the American Civil War.

cx is derived variously from the Scottish *och aye*, the Finnish *oikea* and the Latin *omnia correcta*.

Of all of these, the first is probably the real derivation, a conclusion supported by no less an authority than the British Privy Council. Nearly 100 years after its first recorded use, OK was still causing problems. In 1935, the word became the focus of a Privy Council court case that revolved around a rice merchant's intentions in writing OK with his initials on invoices. Their lordships launched an investigation of the meaning of OK (British judges are notorious for being at least 100 years behind the times concerning popular culture and language), and concluded that 'the letters hail from the U.S.A. and represent a spelling, humorous or uneducated, of the words *All Correct*'.

The Welsh penguin

The earliest recognisable version of the English language is Old English, a Germanic tongue spoken in the north of Germany and introduced into Britain through the Anglo-Saxon invasions. The poem *Beowulf* (probably created around 700 CE and written down around 1000 CE) is the best-known example of Old English.

A quote from the poem shows how much English has changed:

Đa wæs on burgum Beowulf Scyldinga, leof leodcyning, longe þrage folcum gefræge (fæder ellor hwearf, aldor of earde), oþþæt him eft onwoc heah Healfdene

This seemingly foreign language apparently means:

Now Beowulf bode in the burg of the Scyldings, leader beloved, and long he ruled in fame with all folk (since his father had gone away from the world), till awoke an heir, haughty Healfdene

Over the years and especially with the Norman invasion, English slowly changed into the vaguely comprehensible Middle English.

The best-known work of that time is Chaucer's *Canterbury Tales* from the fourteenth century:

Whan that the Knyght had thus his tale ytoold,
In al the route ne was ther yong ne oold
That he ne seyde it was a noble storie.

By the sixteenth century and Shakespeare, Modern English was emerging and most of the language looks familiar to us nowadays, even if not every word is immediately clear:

> *It is Othello's pleasure, our noble and valiant general, that, upon certain tidings now arrived, importing the mere perdition of the Turkish fleet, every man put himself into triumph.*

Since Shakespeare's time, of course, English has continued changing and other languages have had a vast influence. Even though the ultimate source of our language is Germanic Old English, only about half the words we use in English are Germanic; the rest come from a variety of languages, with French and Latin predominating. One reason for the richness of English is its incessant **borrowing** of words from other languages. Indeed, Booker T. Washington has described this constant acquisition of new words from other languages as more than borrowing:

> *We don't just borrow words; on occasion, English has pursued other languages down alleyways to beat them unconscious and rifle their pockets for new vocabulary.*

These borrowings often occur when someone fluent in two languages starts using words from one in the other. When they use such words to someone who only speaks one of the languages, the words clearly sound, and indeed are, foreign.

Even modern English contains many words and phrases that sound foreign, such as *raison d'être* from French and, my favourite, *Paleoweltschmerz* from German (it refers to the theory that the dinosaurs became extinct through sheer boredom with the world). As time passes and these 'foreign' words continue to be used, they become conventionalised and accepted as part of English.

Scandinavian languages had an early influence on borrowings, still seen in the use of *nay*, meaning no, in dialects in the north of England. After the Norman Conquest, French became the main language to be plundered. These adoptions from French often complemented English words, with subtle differences reflecting the social uses of the two languages. French was the language of the aristocracy, the court and officialdom, while English was for rustics. Thus for farm animals, such as *lamb* and *cow*, we use English forms, but their culinary equivalents (*mutton* and *beef*) are derived from French. A rural job like *shepherd* is English, whereas an urban occupation, such as *haberdasher*, is French.

More recently, English has borrowed words from just about every language imaginable. For many of these, the place where the object referred to by the word was first encountered provides a good indication of the likely source language.

Can you guess which language the following words were borrowed from?

tornado	curry
mosque	wombat
bog	tsunami

While Spanish *tornadoes*, Arabic *mosques*, Gaelic *bogs*, Tamil *curries*, Aboriginal Australian *wombats* and Japanese *tsunamis* may be logical, who would ever think that *penguin* may come from Welsh? If you're now wondering why Welsh could be the root for the name of a bird found only in the southern hemisphere, one explanation goes that the Welsh for white head, *pen gwyn*, was originally used by Welsh sailors for the great auk, a now-extinct bird similar to the penguin found in Newfoundland that had a white spot in front of each eye.

Other surprising origins include the Hebrew source of *jubilee*. The Hebrew word *yobhel*, meaning trumpet, is the root here. Originally all slaves were emancipated every 50 years in a ceremony proclaimed by trumpets. This 50-year cycle eventually became a jubilee. Another strange one is the Gaelic *sluagh-ghairm*, literally meaning army call or an Irish battle cry, which over the years became *slogan*.

But perhaps the most bizarre derivation is that of *bizarre* itself. Bearded Spanish soldiers fighting in France made a strange impression on the locals, who used the Basque word *bizar*, meaning beard, to show how odd these soldiers looked. Bizarre was then borrowed from French into English, and a word that originally meant beard came to mean strange.

Wanted: A computer, female, age 18–25

Over the last 30 years, the biggest source of **neologisms** or new words in English has probably been computing. *Internet* first appeared in 1986, for instance, and has since become an everyday word for many people. *E-mail* first appeared in 1982 and *blog* in 1998.

New ideas are not only expressed by coining words. Even more common is adding fresh meanings to existing words. Still within the computing field, the words *mouse, hardware, program, virus* and *monitor* have all taken on new meanings in the last 50 years, but they continue to be used with their original senses – a mouse is still a small rodent as well as a computing device.

When a new meaning is added, however, the original sense is not always retained. A *computer* used to be a role involving lots of longhand addition and subtraction. With the introduction of calculators and machine computers, there was no longer any need for human computers, and the job-related meaning of the word became obsolete. Nowadays, a 1930s recruitment advert such as the one in the title of this chapter sounds very strange.

The meanings of other words have also been dictated by the times. In the Victorian age, *imperialism* and *colonialism* were seen as bright, positive goals for nations. Now they are pejoratives. Similarly, prior to the Second World War *appeasement* was a positive way of avoiding conflict, but now it connotes cowardice.

For other words, especially adjectives, that have gained new meanings, the newer sense steadily takes over from the old. *Gay* is an example of this. The original meaning of lively is now almost lost, although some of the older generation still use the word in this way. Nowadays, gay is far more likely to mean homosexual.

One of the most extreme examples of a word with a **changed meaning** is *egregious*. Originally meaning outstanding or exceptional, a couple of authors used it ironically in discussing problems. This ironic use was taken up by other writers, so that now egregious means conspicuously bad, the complete opposite of its original sense. Other strange changes in meaning include *commonplace*, which also originally meant its opposite – notable – and *lewd*, which used to mean uneducated.

Here are some words that have changed meanings. Can you guess what their original meanings were?

crafty	commendable
fond	lucky
happy	strong
plausible	foolish

While words like *crafty* (from strong to cunning), *fond* (from foolish to affectionate), *happy* (from lucky to cheerful) and *plausible* (from commendable to possible) have only undergone a single change in meaning, some words have been through a whole series of changes. For instance, both *silly* and *nice* have had at least seven distinct meanings at various times. *Silly* originally meant either happy in Old Norse or blessed in Old High German. It shifted sense through pious to innocent at the start of the thirteenth century. Within the next century the meaning changed to harmless, pitiable and then weak, until it reached its current sense of foolish in 1576. The last of these was the original meaning of *nice* around 1290. Over the following 200 years that word changed sense to timid, then fussy, then delicate and then careful. By the mid-eighteenth century nice had the more familiar meaning of agreeable, with the final sense of kind added on in 1830. Perhaps in another 500 years or so, silly will follow nice and change its meaning another seven times to eventually mean kind too.

Who is that word?

One of the best ways to gain a kind of immortality is to have the scientific community name something after you. Most commonly this is the Latin name for an animal or plant, such as the frog *Rhinoderma darwinii*, the fungus *Cyttaria darwinii* or the tree *Lecocarpus darwinii* (although Charles Darwin is in far less need of the extra renown than most of us). Since most people don't use Latinate species names too often, better still would be to get yourself into the common species name, such as *Darwin frog* (yet another mention for the great Victorian biologist) or even *Magnolia*, named after botany professor Pierre Magnol. Alternatively, you could leave biology and aim for another of the sciences. Perhaps a unit of measurement, such as a *joule* or a *newton* (another scientist not needing the fame), would be nice. Or a special molecule would be a neat way of being commemorated, such as *buckminsterfullerene*, which is shaped like the geodesic domes its namesake was famous for.

None of these scientific approaches to nominal immortality is likely to have much impact on everyday life. To be commemorated by millions of people every day, you need to get a normal English word or phrase based on your name. There are a few of these around already.

Who do you think the following were named after?

algorithm	guy
dunce	teddy bear

While the words may be used frequently, the users are often not aware of their roots. After all, who thinks of al-

Khuwarizmi, a ninth-century Arab mathematician, when saying *algorithm*, or of John Duns Scotus, a thirteenth-century Scottish philosopher and (ironically) genius, when using *dunce*, or of Guy Fawkes, infamous for trying to blow up the English Houses of Parliament, as the source of *guy*, or, more recently, of former US President Theodore Roosevelt as the root of *teddy bear*? For people to be fully aware that it is your name that is being commemorated, it's even better to try to get yourself put into an **idiomatic phrase**.

If you hear the name Hobson, you probably immediately think of *Hobson's choice*, which, as a choice of only one, really means no choice. But who was the original Hobson? He was in fact a Cambridge innkeeper who supplied horses to travellers. When someone wanted a horse, the innkeeper would only allow them to take the one that had rested the longest, the result being that there was no real choice.

Who was the source of *his name is mud*? One Dr Samuel Mudd was a Washington doctor who inadvertently set the broken leg of John Wilkes Booth, Abraham Lincoln's assassin, in 1865. His association with the phrase certainly added to its popularity, but in fact its usage goes back at least as far as 1823.

The original Mickey Finn – who presumably was the first to slip someone a *Mickey Finn* – was a disreputable Chicago bar owner. As well as being known as the head of a group of pickpockets, Finn also robbed many of his customers, having first spiked their drinks to put them to sleep. This does make you wonder why anyone would ever go to his bar.

And who was *the real McCoy*? Suggestions range from a Scottish whisky producer called G Mackay who changed the brand name to McCoy for the US, to a Prohibition-era bootlegger called Bill McCoy, an engineer and inventor called Elijah McCoy and the boxer Kid McCoy.

Cornflakes® or cornflakes?

One of the most unusual sources of words is **trademark names**. Companies want their goods to be well known. After all, if when thinking about early-morning foods you think of *cornflakes* rather than *breakfast cereal*, you are more likely to purchase the cereal trademarked Cornflakes® than any other brand. However, there comes a point where the trademark name takes over from the generic word, so that people start referring to all breakfast cereals as cornflakes, and the trademark becomes just one more word in the English language.

Such popularisation of trademark words can cause immense legal difficulties for the companies concerned, as they may lose their exclusive rights to the word – a process neatly termed **genericide**. This is particularly likely when the original trademark starts to be used as a verb. For example, you might *xerox* a page from this book (although the Xerox company has attempted to encourage people to use the verb *photocopy* instead, so that its rights over its name are retained) or maybe *hoover* the carpet between chapters. However you use them, you may be surprised at the number of trademarks in everyday English.

Which of the words below were originally trademarks?

aspirin	concrete
dry ice	escalator
foolscap	jacuzzi
modem	ping-pong

There are interesting little histories behind some words that were originally trademarks. *Heroin*, for instance, was first produced as a medical replacement for morphine and so used to be a company product. *Tabloid* as a trademark referred to a compressed medical tablet. The meaning was then applied to a compressed style of journalism. And *zipper* was originally a trademark for a make of boots with zippers, rather than the fastenings themselves. Along with *aspirin*, *dry ice*, *escalator*, *jacuzzi* and *ping-pong*, these illustrate how trademark names have come to pervade everyday English.

As well as taking care in coming up with names of products, businesspeople also need to think carefully about what they call their companies. With luck, a company name could last for over 1,400 years, as is the case with *Kongo Gumi*, a Japanese construction company founded in 578.

The two most common sources of **company names** are abbreviations and the names of founders. From the *BBC* (British Broadcasting Corporation) and *Nabisco* (National Biscuit Company) to more subtle names such as *Esso* (for S O, Standard Oil) and *Q8* (for Kuwait Petroleum International), abbreviations provide a succinct way of stating key information about a company.

Then there are the original founders who name companies after themselves – Harvey *Firestone*, Henry *Ford*, Soichiro *Honda*, Shozo *Kawasaki* and Glen *Bell*, who founded Taco Bell. There are also company names that combine founders and abbreviations. *Corel* stands for founder Dr Michael COwpland's REsearch Laboratory; *DHL* commemorates the surnames of its three founders, Adrian Dalsey, Larry Hillblom and Robert Lynn; and *IKEA* is short for founder Ingvar Kamprad, his family farm Elmtaryd and a nearby village, Agunnaryd.

Some company names have deep meanings in other languages. *Daewoo* means great universe in Korean, *Hitachi* is sunrise in Japanese, *Nintendo* means heaven blesses hard work in Japanese, and *Volkswagen* is people's car in German. More strangely, *Oreo* is Greek for hill, named so because the cookies were originally mound shaped, and *Volvo* is Latin for I roll. Another Latin word is *Audi*. The founder, August Horch, started a company named after himself but left after five years. Still wanting to manufacture cars, he founded a new company that he also wanted to name after himself. Since his surname was already taken, he translated it (Horch means listen) into Latin for the new company.

There are other idiosyncratic origins of company names. *Coca-Cola* commemorates the coca leaves and kola nuts originally used as flavourings, whereas *Pepsi* alludes to dyspepsia, an ailment the drink was designed to alleviate. *Shell* started off importing seashells, *Starbucks* is named after a character in *Moby Dick*, and both *Lada* and *Nike* commemorate gods. Animals also feature: *Reebok* is an antelope and *Lycos* is short for a family of wolf spiders.

The most peculiar company name of all must be *Fanta*. The drink was originally made from cheese and jam by-products in Second World War Germany. Clearly, a bit of imagination (or *Fantasie* in German) was needed to think that it tasted of oranges.

The makings of fashionable language

We all know that **William Shakespeare** (1564–1616) was the author of some of the most-read plays and poems in the world (albeit that much of this reading is forced on students against their will). With 37 plays, 154 sonnets and a few other assorted poems to his name, the prodigiously productive playwright had a massive influence on the theatre and English literature in general.

What is less well known is Shakespeare's influence on the English language. His entire work contains over 20,000 different words, and some authorities reckon that one in twelve of these was an invented word or gave a fresh meaning to a current term. Shakespeare made up words, added prefixes and suffixes to existing words, combined words and changed nouns into verbs. Given that the first known use of around 1,700 words or meanings is in Shakespeare and that his work has been so widely read, it's not surprising that many of the terms we use every day come from him. When we say something is *fashionable*, *marketable*, *obscene* or *flawed*, when we say someone is *critical*, *generous*, *lonely* or *useless*, and when we talk of *accommodation* or a *bump*, we are using words that Shakespeare originated. His influence is unparalleled.

It's not only in separate words that Shakespeare had such an impact. The number of phrases he invented that are now casually thrown about in everyday use stretches the bounds of credulity. When we talk of *the makings of* something, when we say that something else has *gone full circle* and when we talk about having *seen better days*, we are quoting the Bard. In fact, one of the bigger dictionaries of quotations includes a massive 3,400 entries by Shakespeare.

Of the phrases below, can you guess which ones are said to originate with Shakespeare?

> a foregone conclusion
> a sorry sight
> beyond the pale
> bloody minded
> fair play
> good riddance
> high time
> in stitches
> pigs might fly
> smooth talk

All of them except *beyond the pale* and *pigs might fly*, is the answer. But fortunately for our egos, not everything Shakespeare did came out perfectly. Some of his coinages have not caught on. No one uses words like *conflux* (coming together), *tortive* (twisted) and *vastidity* (immensity). And his grammar at times could do with some brushing up – the *most unkindest cut of all* is but one example. Nevertheless, as the individual who has had the most influence on English, he is far ahead of anyone else.

The origin of phrases

The **origin of phrases** is a fascinating area full of surprises. Some are understandable, such as *having egg on your face* from the tradition of throwing eggs at bad performers. Others are less straightforward. *Dead as a door nail*, for instance, dates from the time when nails were very expensive and had to be reused whenever possible. Nails that held a door needed to be bent back and so could not be reused, and thus door nails were dead. Another strange phrase is *pay through the nose*, which may have originated in a ninth-century tax law imposed on Ireland by the conquering Danes, which included the provision of slitting the noses of tax evaders.

Many other idioms are similarly ancient. Both *hair of the dog* and *living in cloud cuckoo land* date back to around 400 BCE and the Greek poet Aristophanes. *Let sleeping dogs lie* is derived from Chaucer in 1374, and *a needle in a haystack* comes from *Don Quixote* by Miguel de Cervantes in 1605.

Some seemingly obscure idioms have picturesque origins. At first it is unclear why, in the phrase *steal someone's thunder*, anyone would own thunder that could be stolen. The reason comes from the playwright John Dennis in 1709. He invented a way of creating the sound of thunder in one of his plays. Unfortunately the play was a flop, but other theatrical producers copied his thunder effect, or stole his thunder. Another interestingly opaque idiom is *kick the bucket*. This has nothing to do with people standing on upside-down buckets before they hang themselves. Rather, bucket is said to be a corruption of *buchet*, or a beam in a slaughterhouse to which pigs were tied before their throats were cut. As they bled to death, the pigs would kick the buchet.

The origins of other phrases are more prosaic. *Not enough room to swing a cat* seems odd until you realise that the cat refers to a cat-o'-nine-tails, or a whip used to discipline sailors. *Tit for tat* is believed to be a corruption of tip for tap, meaning a blow for a blow.

Of other intriguing idioms, *buy the farm* (to die) dates from the First World War, when the US government sent enough money to purchase a small farm to the family of any soldier killed in combat. *Pass the buck* (to avoid responsibility) comes from card games that use a marker called a buck to show who has responsibility for dealing. *The third degree* originates in Masonic lodges, where there are three degrees of initiation. To enter the third degree entails lengthy and challenging questioning.

Lastly, *cock and bull story* (an exaggerated, deceptive tale) is possibly a corruption of 'concocted and bully story', *bully* being an old word for exaggerated. The word *bull* meaning nonsense is actually a venerable term dating from around 1300, and is the root of *bullshit*, which is why we don't say cowshit or pigshit instead.

The **etymology** of other idioms is a matter of some dispute. Probably the most controversial phrase is *the whole nine yards*. Explanations for its origin include the length of a Second World War ammunition belt, the amount of fabric needed for a suit or a kilt, the amount of concrete in a concrete mixer, the number of sails on a sailing ship, and the distance needed to be gained to earn a first down in American football (that is actually ten yards, so the phrase would be used ironically to indicate you hadn't quite made it). There is little evidence justifying any of the explanations.

For other phrases there is one clearly identifiable origin, but the waters have been muddied by suggestions of other spurious explanations that take on a life of their own. For instance, *bite the bullet* comes from the desperate and painful battlefield surgery prior to the invention of anaesthetics. To prevent patients biting through their own tongue, a bullet was placed in their mouth before the surgeon started work. It has, however, been erroneously suggested that the phrase has origins in the Indian Mutiny in the nineteenth century. At that time, prior to firing a musket, waxed-paper cartridges needed to be torn with the teeth. A rumour started that the cartridges had been waxed using either pork fat (offending Muslims) or beef fat (offending Hindus), making biting the bullet an unpleasant task for the soldiers. Unfortunately it was not bullets that came in waxed cartridges but gunpowder, so there's no truth in the tale.

An even more ludicrous pseudo-explanation involves *dead ringer*, which apparently concerns burying a bell with a corpse to allow the dead person to signal for aid if they revived. This picturesque story unfortunately ignores the facts that a bell cannot be heard through six feet of earth and that someone buried alive in a coffin would quickly suffocate. The real explanation for dead ringer is far less interesting. The word *ringer* has been used in horseracing to mean a substituted horse for over 100 years, and *dead* can mean exact, as in dead centre and dead shot, so a dead ringer is merely an exact substitute.

There are other idioms where a suggested explanation is a true story but is not the origin of the phrase. For *white elephant* (a burdensome possession), nineteenth-century circus owner P. T. Barnum did buy an expensive white elephant, but when it arrived it was covered with pink blotches and was therefore useless. However, the true origins of the phrase lie in ancient Burmese and Thai tradition. Captured rare white elephants were considered sacred and needed special and costly attention. If any nobleman displeased the king, he would be given the dubious honour of having to look after a white elephant, a task so expensive that it could easily be ruinous.

Part II
Pronunciation and Spelling

Orthography, n. The science of spelling by the eye instead of the ear. Advocated with more heat than light by the out-mates of every asylum for the insane.
                    Ambrose Bierce, The Devil's Dictionary

nglish's most notorious shortcoming is its annoyingly inconsistent spelling. Strictly, it's not just the spelling that's the problem, but the mismatches between spellings and pronunciations. Irrespective of how they're spelt, the pronunciations of some words sound pleasant while others grate on our ears, and strings of words with similar sounds can either add to the glories of English or make some sentences nigh on impossible to speak. All in all, the sounds and spellings of English are a fascinating area worthy of a closer look.

Mispellings (sic)

E nglish is a fiendishly tricky language to spell. For most people, **misspellings** (not mispellings) abound. Probably the most commonly committed misspellings are grammatical in nature rather than indicating a lack of knowledge of how to spell a particular word. *Its* is confused with *it's*, while *there*, *their* and *they're* are sometimes used seemingly at random.

Nevertheless, the notoriety of English spelling lies in the hundreds of words that could perfectly reasonably be spelt in at least two different ways. Why do we have *millennium* but *millenarian*? Why is it *cemetery* and not *cemetary*? The vagaries of English spelling are perhaps best illustrated by George Bernard Shaw's spelling of fish as *ghoti* (using the *gh* in enough, the *o* in women, and the *ti* in nation). The problems really become apparent when you realise that fish could also be spelt as *pheesi*, *pfuchsi*, *ſtiapsh* and even *ueisci* (sorry, you'll have to work out for yourself where these come from).

The reasoning behind most of these spellings comes down to the word's etymology. English has borrowed thousands of words from other languages and, in a somewhat uptight manner, prefers to retain spellings close to the original rather than respell the words to fit its own conventions. For example, for the annoyingly inconsistent *-able* and *-ible* endings to words (think of *abominable* and *convertible*), if the root Latin verb is one ending *-ere* or *-ire*, then *-ible* is used, whereas if the Latin root is *-are* the ending is *-able*. For the *-er/-or* problem (*abductor* but *decanter*), if the full word exists in Latin it is spelt with *-or*, but if the word is created from an existing English verb it is spelt *-er*.

These attempts to mirror the spellings of the original languages were taken too far, however. Some sixteenth-century scholars decided to make English spelling even more complicated than it already was by changing the spellings of words to indicate their roots, so both *debt* and *doubt* had extra *b*s added to reflect their Latin origins.

Knowing the roots of spelling conventions like these is all well and good, but it is somewhat unreasonable to expect people to have to learn the tens of languages that English has borrowed from, including several dead languages, just to be able to spell correctly. After all, these multiple origins of words have led to a situation where the single vowel sound *ee* can be spelt in at least eight different ways:

He believed Caesar could see people seizing the stormy seas.

No wonder there have been numerous calls for spelling reform over the years.

A constant thorn for people trying to spell English correctly is whether a single or double consonant should be used in the middle of a word. We've already seen this with *millennium* and *millenarian*, but it reaches its apogee in the pair of words *committee* and *comity*. Other tricky words include *desiccated* but *moccasin*, and *inoculate* but *innocuous*.

Another spelling problem concerns a few unusual spellings that are reminiscent of other more easily spelt words.

How many of the following words are misspelt? And what are the correct spellings?

aquaduct	concensus
miniscule	momento
sacreligious	supercede

While all the strange spellings in English may appear ridiculous, it's a much better situation now than when printing started. With no widely accepted conventions at the time, people (or, as the word could then be spelt, *poepull* or *pupyll* or *pepule*) were free to spell words any way they wanted. So receive could be *rasawe*, *rescheyve* or *ressayf*, and church could be *chrch*, *schorche* or *sscherch*. The record holder was probably *through*, which Melvyn Bragg points out had over 500 possible spellings. Perhaps we should be happy that there are conventions nowadays, even if these include such oddities as *aqueduct*, *consensus*, *minuscule*, *memento*, *sacrilegious* and *supersede*. Even now, however, variants are possible. *Minuscule* is so frequently misspelt *miniscule* that the latter has become a possible form of the word, and it seems likely that *supercede* will also become acceptable in the near future because of the frequency of the traditionally incorrect spelling.

Why is 'colonel' pronounced 'kernel'?

Much of the blame for the difficulties of English spelling really lies with its **pronunciation** rather than its spelling. When a word is not pronounced the way it is spelt, is it the spelling or the pronunciation that causes the difference? Most often the fault is with the pronunciation.

Once a word has been written down, its spelling is set and unlikely to change. Spoken language, on the other hand, is ephemeral and pronunciations change over time. So while the spelling remains constant, the original pronunciation that matched the spelling drifts to something different, and a yawning gap may open between the two.

The best-known change in English pronunciation is the Great Vowel Shift, such a massive alteration that the name warrants capital letters. This was a series of sound changes, the reason for which isn't clear, but similar shifts occur in many languages at various points in their history. Prior to the GVS, which took place over around 200 years, Chaucer rhymed *food*, *good* and *blood* (sounding similar to *goad*). With Shakespeare, after the GVS, the three words still rhymed, although by that time all of them rhymed with *food*. More recently, *good* and *blood* have independently shifted their pronunciations again.

Similarly, *-ough* in English gains its infamy because of shifts in pronunciation, the same shifts as happened to *-igh* and *-aught*. Originally *night* sounded something like the German word *nicht*, but over time the sound given to the *gh* changed. A similar set of changes, although somewhat more extreme, affected *-ough*, so that now it has nine possible pronunciations, as shown in the following sentence.

A rough-coated, dough-faced, thoughtful ploughman strode through Scarborough; after falling into a slough, he coughed and hiccoughed.

The traditional spelling of the last word is *hiccupped*, but over-generalisation of the applicability of *-ough* resulted in *hiccough*.

In contrast to these cases where a single spelling can be articulated in many different ways, there are also occasions where different spellings have the same pronunciation. For example, originally *bird*, *hurt* and *fern* were enunciated following the second letter of the word, but over time the sounds converged.

These changes in pronunciation can be seen by reading old poems and plays. For instance, Alexander Pope in the eighteenth century rhymed *obey* and *tea*. And Shakespeare's Falstaff made a pun on *reason* and *raisin*, since at that time both words were pronounced like the latter.

Perhaps the best exposition of the problems of English pronunciation is a poem entitled 'The Chaos' by G. Nolst Trenité in the early twentieth century. It starts:

Dearest creature in creation
Studying English pronunciation,
I will teach you in my verse
Sounds like corpse, corps, horse and worse
I will keep you, Susy, busy,
Make your head with heat grow dizzy.
Tear in eye, your dress you'll tear,
Queer, fair seer, hear my prayer,
Pray, console your loving poet,
Make my coat look new, dear, sew it!

A later verse of the poem runs:

Rally with ally; yea, ye,
Eye, I, ay, aye, whey, key, quay!
Say aver, but ever, fever.
Neither, leisure, skein, receiver.

In this verse you'll notice the words *I* and *eye* – two words with the same pronunciation but no letters in common. Two more pairs of words with the same characteristic are *you* and *ewe*, and *oh* and *eau*. These are **homophones**, words that are pronounced the same but spelt differently.

Another illustration of the extreme inconsistencies of English spelling and pronunciation comes in **homographs**. These are words that can be pronounced in two separate ways without changing the spelling. So, for example, *wind* can mean either moving air or to twist or wrap, and the pronunciation is different depending on the meaning. Similarly, the past tense of wind is *wound*, but with a different pronunciation the latter can mean an injury. A *tear* as a rip or eye water has two pronunciations, as does *resume* depending on whether it means continue or curriculum vitae (in the latter case it should strictly be written *résumé*, but the accents are generally dropped).

Can you think of homographs with the following pairs of meanings?
> a motorbike *or* was gloomy
> part of a fish *or* a liquid measure
> a way of serving a meal *or* to blow
> part of a musical instrument *or* to bend at the waist
> small *or* a unit of time
> a drain *or* a tailor

And finally, if you've been wondering why *colonel* is pronounced *kernel*, it all comes down to its origin in the Italian word *colonna*. This Italian rank was first adopted by the French, who changed the *l* to an *r*. English borrowed the word from French, keeping the *r* pronunciation, but later switching the spelling back to *l* to get closer to the Italian root. This just goes to show that a single word with a single pronunciation can be at least as intriguing and odd as the strange homographs *moped, gill, buffet, bow, minute* and *sewer.*

Sounds good to me

One of the weirdest things about language is the lack of any relationship between the sound of most words and their meaning. To many people's ears, the word *good* probably doesn't sound particularly good, while *malevolent* (at least to me) has quite a pleasant ring to it. There's no real reason for the way over 99 per cent of words sound. The connections we make between certain sounds and meanings are just conventions, and as long as everyone accepts that certain combinations of sounds have certain meanings, things work out OK and people can talk to each other.

There is, nevertheless, a tiny set of words where the sound does link to the meaning. In **onomatopoeia**, the word sounds like the thing it is describing. So snakes *hiss*, with the *ss* mirroring the noise that snakes actually make. Clearly, however, there are limits to things in the world that make sounds that can be translated into onomatopoeia. What does a *house* sound like? Or what noise should be associated with *believe*? Or even what sound does *sound* make?

Even though there is no relationship between sound and meaning for the overwhelming majority of words, the sounds may still conjure up images. Some words seem warm and comfortable; others appear harsh and cold. Personally, I think *bamboozle* has a lovely sound to it, while *crepuscular* is not something I would like to be described as, purely based on the sound of the word. (I had to look up crepuscular in a dictionary to find out what it means – 'pertaining to twilight' isn't that bad, but it doesn't stop me disliking the sound of the word.)

This emotive characteristic of words has led to several surveys of both the most beautiful words in English and the worst sounding. Poets and other writers, teachers of speech and the general public have all been asked for their opinions. The most beautiful words identified in these surveys include *anemone, golden, marigold, mist, thrush, gossamer, lullaby, luminous* and *tendril,* while some of the worst-sounding words are *crunch, flatulent, jazz, jukebox, sap, cacophonous, fructify, gargoyle, plump* and *plutocrat.*

Whether the sounds of words (at least in English) are rated positively or negatively seems to depend on a couple of aspects:

- ∞ Words whose sounds flow smoothly (and thus require the tongue to move about in the mouth only a little) are preferred, whereas words with abrupt short sounds or requiring complicated tongue movements to say them are disliked.
- ∞ Words with soft consonants (e.g. *l, m, s*) are preferred to words with hard consonants (e.g. *g, k*).

Of all the people who have stated a preference or dislike for certain words, probably the most influential in terms of English literature is James Joyce. The famous Irish author of *Ulysses* and *Finnegans Wake,* who was renowned for his preoccupation with obscure vocabulary, chose *cuspidor* as the single most beautiful word in English. While the sound of the word, at least to his ears, may be nice, the meaning isn't quite so pleasant – a cuspidor is a spittoon.

A cheerful but challenging chapter

The title of this chapter is an example of **alliteration** – the use of the same initial consonant (or pair of consonants) in successive words. Alliteration is most commonly associated with poetry. For example, William Wordsworth wrote:

> And sings a solitary song
> That whistles in the wind.

In the first of these two lines words starting with s are dominant, and in the second the key words start with w.

Alliteration is more than merely a poetic technique. Alliterative phrases are catchy and so easier to remember. They are therefore often favoured by companies in naming products (e.g. *Coca-Cola*) and, indeed, by anyone wanting to make a phrase more memorable. Just think of Walt Disney's most famous characters: *Mickey Mouse, Minnie Mouse* and *Donald Duck*.

Alliteration also plays a role in everyday English, with phrases and idioms often being alliterative. *It takes two to tango* trips off the tongue more readily than *it takes two to waltz*. And when we feel *hale and hearty* and the *sweet smell of success* is near, we *jump for joy*.

With so many alliterative phrases in English, can you complete the following?

Back to...	Boom or...
A dime a...	Green as...
The more the...	

Another common use of alliteration is in nursery rhymes and **tongue twisters**. The best-known tongue twister in English relies on alliteration:

Peter Piper picked a peck of pickled peppers.

And I guess we could use alliterative phrases like *back to basics, boom or bust, a dime a dozen, green as grass* and *the more the merrier* as the basis for other similar tongue twisters.

More difficult tongue twisters can be created through double alliteration, where two starting consonants alternate. As we start getting used to saying one initial consonant, it suddenly switches to another and trips us up. A famous example of this type is:

She sells seashells on the seashore.

This double alliteration is also the root of the problems with pronouncing some even more challenging tongue twisters, such as:

The sixth sick sheikh's sixth sheep's sick.

On a final note, not all tongue twisters work in this way. The trickiest include pairs of adjacent consonants that require us to completely reshape our mouth very quickly. For instance:

Peggy Babcock (try saying the name five times quickly)
Mrs Smith's Fish Sauce Shop

Part III

Usage

*Usage, n. The First Person of the literary Trinity, the Second
and Third being Custom and Conventionality. Imbued with a
decent reverence for this Holy Triad an industrious writer may
hope to produce books that will live as long as the fashion.*

Ambrose Bierce, The Devil's Dictionary*

W e use language unthinkingly every day. Most of
the time we rely primarily on a limited set of
common words, which we intersperse with more
unusual terms. We don't all use language in the same way,
however. While each of us has our own curious peccadilloes
(one of mine, at least in writing, is frequently starting sentences with *while*), more noticeable are the differences between
varieties of English, such as between British and American
English – 'You say tomayto, I say tomahto.'

Irrespective of the variety we speak, to avoid long-
windedness we use abbreviations, we succinctly create
nuggets of truth with proverbs, and we make our language
more picturesque by employing sobriquets, although we also
run the risk of overdoing things with clichés. Our use of
English can also say a lot about who we are – what things we
like to avoid mentioning directly and replace with
euphemisms, how we try to avoid giving offence by employing politically correct language, and what social groups we
associate with through our slang. With such potential for
insights, English usage is a rich and fertile area for exploration.

The of to in

English probably has more words than any other language, by various estimates between 750,000 and a million. In contrast, French is said to have around 200,000 words.

Figures like these should be treated with caution for several reasons. One is that it's not really clear what is meant by 'one word'. Presumably *set* is a word, but should we count *sets* and *setting* as separate words? What about the more than 120 separate meanings of *set* listed in the *Oxford English Dictionary*? What about phrasal verbs such as *set off* and *set to*? Are these separate words?

It's also important to consider what counts as an English word. Should we include words that haven't been used since the sixteenth century? Or words that are only used in the north of Scotland? What about the Cantonese word *gweilo*, commonly used in Hong Kong English to describe foreigners (as white devils) and found in quite a few books? What about abbreviations, or the vast number of words now being coined and spread via the internet? Whatever is decided, English is definitely the language with the richest vocabulary.

Despite the vast number of words in English, we tend to use only a small proportion in everyday language. Most novels, for example, contain fewer than 10,000 different words, while Shakespeare used over 20,000 different words in his complete works (again, this depends on how you count one word). The record for variety is probably held by James Joyce, who used over 50,000 different words in the novel *Finnegans Wake*, albeit most of these words he made up.

Using a range of vocabulary like James Joyce's is out of the question for most people. Indeed, we rely heavily on a few **common words**. In many texts, 7 per cent of the total number of terms are occurrences of *the*, while the top ten most frequent words often make up 25 per cent of a text. What these top ten words are is debatable, since different lists can be created by counting the frequency of terms in various texts. Here are three typical top ten lists for written English.

the	the	the
of	of	of
to	and	and
in	to	to
and	in	a
a	a	in
for	is	is
was	that	that
is	be	was
that	it	it

You may notice that these words don't carry much meaning in themselves. Rather, they provide the links between the meaningful words. Such terms are called **function words**.

Similar to the lists of top ten words in written English, lists can also be constructed for spoken English. While many of the words in the two top tens are the same, lists of the most common words in spoken English contain two that do not appear in those for written English: *I* and *you*.

Whatever the top ten, one thing that's noticeable is that shorter words dominate, a feature common to all languages. Indeed, in all of the top tens there is only one four-letter word, namely *that*.

One final interesting issue concerning word frequencies is the idea that if we generally rely on only a small sample of all the possible words we could use, why not reduce English to a much smaller size and get rid of all these thousands of terms that are almost never used? This was the rationale behind the proposals for **Basic English**, created by Charles Kay Ogden in the 1930s. Basic English was an attempt to reduce the vocabulary of the language to only 850 words (100 operators such as *come*, *about* and *but*; 600 words for things; and 150 words for qualities). While this may seem laudable, a quick look at the Gettysburg Address in Basic English reveals its limitations:

Seven and eighty years have gone by from the day when our fathers gave to this land a new nation – a nation which came to birth in the thought that all men are free, a nation given up to the idea that all men are equal.

In case you don't know it, the original is:

Four score and seven years ago our fathers brought forth, upon this continent, a new nation, conceived in liberty, and dedicated to the proposition that 'all men are created equal'.

The Basic English version doesn't seem any easier to read. Indeed, replacing *ago* with the convoluted phrase *have gone by from the day when* makes it more difficult. Rather than trying to control and simplify the language, we should be happy with the richness of English, revel in its oddities and absurdities, and celebrate its variety.

Divided by a common language

Winston Churchill is once supposed to have said that Britain and America were 'two countries divided by a common language' (the attribution is actually uncertain, as George Bernard Shaw previously stated that they were 'two countries separated by the same language'). While there are other important varieties of the tongue, **British and American English** remain the two dominant forces, and they are noticeably different. The divergence is apparent at four levels: pronunciation, spelling, grammar and vocabulary.

For pronunciation, there is so much variation within each of the two countries that generalising differences between them is difficult. Nevertheless, some patterns emerge. For example, Americans are likely to omit the *y* sound (strictly in linguistic terms a /j/) attached to certain consonants. Thus to British ears it may sound as if an American is saying:

They sing toons and eat stoo while reading the noospaper on Toosday.

More noticeably, the pronunciation of some words differs. In America people have *leesure* time, while in Britain they have *lesure* time. Americans eat *tomaytoes* with *orregano* while Brits eat *tomahtoes* (but still consume *potaytoes*) with *oregahno*. Americans prefer to give the full sound to all the syllables in *secretary* and *laboratory*, while Brits are lazier in saying *secretry* and *laboratry*. These differences are fairly minor, however, and both Americans and Brits may have more trouble understanding a strong regional accent from their own country than a standard accent from the other country. They have the most trouble understanding a strong accent from the other nation, as evinced by the need for subtitles for US television programmes when people with a strong regional British accent are speaking.

Spelling differences between the two countries are also minor. You spell *favor*, I spell *favour*; you spell *recognize*, I spell *recognise* (you may have noted from the spellings I have used in this book that I'm British). Some American spellings are taking over, so that many Brits now do not double the *s* in, say, *focusing*, as they are supposed to do.

Grammatical differences also have little impact on mutual comprehension, as they are restricted to a few odd points. Americans are less likely to use the past perfect tense (*I had done*) than Brits, and more likely to use *I don't have* rather than the British *I haven't got* – indeed, the last word would often be *gotten* in US English.

It's when we come to vocabulary differences between the two varieties that the chances for mutual misunderstanding become high. *Biscuits* in Britain are *cookies* in America, while American *biscuits* are British *scones*, and asking for *chips* to go with a sandwich could result in you receiving either *French fries* in Britain or the equivalent of British *crisps* in America. Saying *He wore a purple vest over his shirt* in Britain is odd, since a British *vest* is an American *undershirt*, whereas an American *vest* is a British *waistcoat*.

For the following British words, what are the American equivalents?

nappy	hoarding
treacle	pack of cards
silencer (of a car)	fringe (of hair)

For the following American words, what are the British equivalents?

eggplant	thumb tack
faucet	hood (of a car)
trunk (of a car)	private school

While most of the differences should just lead to blank stares, a few could cause embarrassment. A Brit saying *Keep your pecker up* might want to know that *pecker* is American slang for penis. Similarly, the American *She landed on her fanny* (meaning her backside) could elicit surprise from Brits, for whom *fanny* is a different part of the female anatomy. For the other way round, a British teacher asking American students for the loan of a *rubber* would probably elicit astonishment at being asked for a condom rather than the desired eraser.

Such embarrassing misunderstandings are fortunately few and far between. The number of concepts expressed in different ways in British and American English is a tiny proportion of the total vocabulary. While we occasionally get confused over *nappy* and *diaper*, *hoarding* and *billboard*, *treacle* and *molasses*, *pack* and *deck*, *silencer* and *muffler*, *fringe* and *bangs*, *eggplant* and *aubergine*, *thumb tack* and *drawing pin*, *faucet* and *tap*, *hood* and *bonnet*, *trunk* and *boot*, and *private school* and *public school*, the overwhelming majority of words have the same meaning on the two sides of the Atlantic.

Given the amount of cross-fertilisation between the cultures through music, films (or movies), literature, sports and so on, it seems likely that the two varieties will remain mutually comprehensible for the foreseeable future.

TCIWR: This Chapter Is Worth Reading

We all prefer an easy life. When pronouncing words we often take the easiest route, so *want to* sounds like *wanna*, *itinerary* is pronounced as a four-syllable word and *handbag* usually comes out as *hambag*. The same preference for simplicity is behind many **abbreviations**. Why say *advertisement* when *advert* or even *ad* will do? And why run the danger of getting your tongue in a twist with *Acquired Immune Deficiency Syndrome* or *deoxyribonucleic acid* when you can get away with *AIDS* and *DNA*?

These examples show the three main types of abbreviations. Advert is a **shortened word**, AIDS is an **acronym** and DNA is an **initialism**.

Some words are used so frequently as shortened forms that unless we really think about it, we don't realise they are abbreviations. We may casually use the word *zoo* without necessarily being conscious that it is short for zoological gardens, we say *fax* without thinking of facsimile, *pants* without worrying about pantaloons and *scrum* while unconcerned about scrummage. This reliance on shortened words is particularly noticeable in Australian English, a key feature of which is the use of diminutives such as *barbie* (for barbecue) and *arvo* (for afternoon).

Do you know the full forms of these shortened words?

bus	cab
cello	sub

Shortened words have become so familiar that in most situations using the full form sounds positively wrong. We're used to talking about *bird flu*, but what is *bird influenza*? How often do we talk about taking the *omnibus* or a *cabriolet*, or about playing the *violoncello*? There are, however, some situations where even Australians may need to use the full form of a shortened word. If the context isn't clear, just saying *sub* could lead to confusion between submarines, subordinates, subscriptions and substitutes.

The second type of abbreviation is the acronym (although the term acronym is also used as an equivalent to abbreviation, rather than just one type of abbreviation). An acronym is a pronounceable word formed from the initial letters of the abbreviated words. So in the international arena we find *NATO*, *UNCTAD* and *UNESCO*.

A very early acronym is the use of the Greek term *ichthus* for Jesus, derived from the initial letters of the Greek words for Jesus Christ, God's Son, Saviour. More recently, some acronyms have become so commonplace that we forget their origins. For instance *scuba* (self-contained underwater breathing apparatus) and *laser* (light amplification by stimulated emission of radiation), originally acronyms, have become words in their own right with no need for capitals. One particularly strange group is recursive acronyms, beloved of the computing community. So *GNU* stands for GNU's Not Unix, and *WINE* stands for Wine Is Not an Emulator.

An initialism is an abbreviation where each of the names of the individual letters is pronounced. Frequently employed to denote government agencies (e.g. *FBI*) and technical terms (e.g. *HTML*), initialisms were traditionally written with a full stop after each letter. So we had the U.S.A. fighting the Cold War against the U.S.S.R. Nowadays the capital letters in the names are taken as being sufficient in themselves to indicate an initialism, so today we write about the *CIA* and the *KGB*.

According to the *Guinness Book of World Records*, the longest initialism recorded is the 56-letter *NIIOMT-PLABOPARMBETZHELBETRABSBOMONIMONKONOT-DTEKHSTROMONT*, a Soviet-era term standing for the laboratory for shuttering, reinforcing, concrete and ferro-concrete operations etc., etc. Fortunately most initialisms are not that long, but they are becoming more common. Kentucky Fried Chicken has officially changed its name to *KFC* and British Petroleum is now *BP*, suggesting a general social acceptance of initialisms.

Some abbreviations fall between initialisms and acronyms. A few, such as *VAT* (standing for Value Added Tax), can be pronounced as a word or spelt out. Others combine the two forms. For instance *JPEG* (standing for Joint Photographic Experts Group) starts with an initial and then has a three-letter acronym.

A chapter a day keeps the word blues away

Proverbs, or well-known wise sayings, are a familiar part of language. We all recognise and may sometimes use proverbs such as:

- ✦ Don't put the cart before the horse.
- ✦ Don't look a gift horse in the mouth.
- ✦ You can lead a horse to water but you can't make it drink.

As can be seen from the prevalence of horses in these examples, most proverbs date back hundreds of years. Indeed, many are actually translations of Latin or Greek equivalents.

The longevity of proverbs lies in the way they provide a concise expression for a nugget of commonly held wisdom. Most of these sayings give sound ethical advice, provide justifications for accepted behaviour, or contain warnings against inappropriate actions. Since much appropriate behaviour is cross-cultural, a widely accepted idea can often be expressed as a proverb in several different languages. For example, the benefits of laughter can be found encapsulated in sayings from a wide range of countries. In French, *a day is lost if one has not laughed*. In Chinese, *you will never be punished for making people die of laughter*. And in Japanese, *time spent laughing is time spent with the gods*.

One problem with proverbs is that what constitutes appropriate behaviour often depends on the situation. So as well as being able to find a proverb that is applicable to pretty well any situation you might want to justify, it's also possible that sayings directly contradict each other.

Can you think of proverbs that contradict the ones below?
> Many hands make light work.
>
> The bigger, the better.
>
> Actions speak louder than words.
>
> A man without words is a man without thoughts.
>
> Life is what you make it.

How about:
> Too many cooks spoil the broth.
>
> The best things come in small packages.
>
> The pen is mightier than the sword.
>
> Silence is golden.
>
> Whatever will be will be.

Many proverbs have been used so frequently that they are in danger of becoming clichés. As with any cliché, this means that the proverbs can be ridiculed, which has led to the creation of perverse proverbs, or **perverbs** for short.

Perverbs generally fall into one of three categories. Some rework the proverb so that it states the blindingly obvious:

∞ All that glitters is not dull.

∞ See a pin and pick it up, and all day long you'll have a pin.

Other perverbs play with the language and force you to re-read the rewritten proverb before you can understand it:

∞ Don't count your chickens will do it for you.

Lastly, there are perverbs that change some of the words in the proverb to give a wholly new meaning, such as the following from noted wit Dorothy Parker (who was asked to construct a sentence using the word 'horticulture'):

∞   You can lead a whore to culture, but you can't make her think.

Another recent trend is that many modern proverbs have been coined as 'laws', rather than being left as authorless expressions. Most famous is Murphy's Law: *If anything can go wrong, it will.* Also well known is Parkinson's Law: *Work expands so as to fill the time available for its completion.* And then there are the amusing pseudo-laws, such as the Gerrold's Laws of Infernal Dynamics:

1   An object in motion will be moving in the wrong direction.
2   An object at rest will be in the wrong place.
3   The energy required to move an object in the correct direction, or put it in the right place, will be more than you wish to expend but not so much as to make the task impossible.

The mother of all chapters

People like assigning **nicknames**. In English-speaking countries many nicknames are a shortening of the real name. So Christine or Christopher becomes *Chris*, and Anthony becomes *Tony*. In some other cultures, many people have a nickname given to them in addition to their real name and the two are not necessarily related. So in Thailand you may meet someone called *Big* because as a baby they were larger than normal, or someone called *Bird* because a bird flew into a window while their mother was pregnant.

There is another longer kind of nickname called a **sobriquet**, which is a picturesque way of highlighting some key characteristic. So William Shakespeare becomes the *Bard of Avon*, indicating his profession and birthplace, and baseball's Babe Ruth, again denoting his profession, is the *Sultan of Swat*. For some reason such sobriquets are particularly favoured by boxers, with Roberto *Hands of Stone* Duran and Mike *The Body-Snatcher* McCullum typical. In fact one boxer, *Marvelous* Marvin Hagler, was so enamoured by his sobriquet that he added it to his real name by deed poll, which makes it unclear whether Marvelous is still a nickname or not.

It is not only people like Napoleon Bonaparte (the *Little Corporal*), the Duke of Wellington (the *Iron Duke*), Abraham Lincoln (the *Great Emancipator*), King Richard I of England (*Coeur de Lion*), King Louis XIV of France (the *Sun King*) and Simon Bolivar (*El Libertador*) who get given sobriquets. Perhaps even more common are nicknames for places: Ireland is the *Emerald Isle*, and Australia is the *Land Down Under*.

One type of sobriquet for cities is for those that term themselves capitals of the world. Thus Aalsmeer in the

Netherlands calls itself the *Flower Capital of the World*, while two towns, Holtville in California and Ohakune in New Zealand, are apparently contesting the title of *Carrot Capital of the World*. Rather less impressively, Sturgis, Michigan wishes to be known as the *Curtain Rod Capital of the World* and Apopka, Florida claims the *Indoor Foliage Capital of the World*. Most intriguing is Knoxville, Tennessee, which apparently is the *Streaking Capital of the World*.

A second frequently used sobriquet for towns concerns canals. Nearly any town or city with a reasonable number of canals wishes to be known as the *Venice of the North*, *South*, *East* or *West* as applicable. At least ten towns lay claim to being the *Venice of the North*, including Birmingham (in England), Stockholm and Hamburg.

Finally, many cities like to be described as the city of something. So Chicago is the *City of Big Shoulders*, Prague is the *City of One Hundred Spires*, Rome is the *City of the Seven Hills*, Paris is the *City of Love*, and Jerusalem is, rather ironically, the *City of Peace*, from the association of the second half of its name with the Hebrew word for peace, *shalom*.

A sobriquet is a two-edged sword, however. Used sparingly, such nicknames can add variety and interest to writing; overused, they are dull and boring, and some have become clichés.

A chapter of epidemic proportions

In the *heated debate* concerning the qualities of good writing, critics have *voiced concern* over the use of **clichés**. A *bitter disappointment* to lovers of good writing, the use of clichés has been increasing *in leaps and bounds*, with writers from *all walks of life* jumping *on the bandwagon* to the extent that the predictable writing of the *rank and file* now *reigns supreme*.

Sorry, that's enough. I'll try to avoid using too many clichés from now on. A cliché, *as if you didn't already know* (oh dear, I've started again), is an overused, trite expression. When coined, most clichés probably struck readers as a neat and unusual way of conveying an idea. The expression was copied over and over, until eventually it became commonplace and even hackneyed. What had once been a clever turn of phrase had turned into a cliché that was used by writers without thinking. Why do *mercies* have to be *tender*? Why is *ignorance* so often *blissful*? Why are *beliefs* nearly always *cherished*? And why do so many people refer to money as *filthy lucre*?

Perhaps the profession most guilty of overusing clichés is journalism. The media are full of hackneyed phrases (admittedly, it is difficult to produce original writing under the extreme pressures of time facing many journalists). The following spoof newspaper article contains several clichés. How many can you identify?

Fire swept through the tree-lined streets of the leafy suburb of Edgetown in the dim hours of the early morning. Driven by a storm packing 50-mph winds, the fire has left the manicured lawns of the suburb strewn with charred rubble. Concerned residents fled on foot in the early-morning hours. Fortunately, in the pre-dawn darkness torrential rain prevented the fire from reaching a densely wooded area. In the wake of the fire, local resident, Amy Bee, faced the gut-wrenching realisation that is every parent's worst nightmare. Her 17-year-old son was missing in the face of Mother Nature's wrath. Later, his charred corpse was pulled from the ashes of their palatial home. In this emergency situation of crisis proportions, she is choked with emotion and struggling to make sense of the tragedy. In an outpouring of support, her neighbours, shocked and saddened, have said that they are on hand to help her deal with her grief.

Clichés can take many forms. Perhaps the most common is the overuse of a particular adjective with a noun, such as *tree-lined streets, leafy suburbs, dim* or *early-morning hours, manicured lawns, charred rubble* or *corpse, concerned* or *local residents, pre-dawn darkness, torrential rain, densely wooded area, gut-wrenching realisation, palatial home, emergency situation* and *crisis proportions*. Other nouns may be preceded by a possessor: the *worst nightmare* often belongs to *every parent*, and *wrath* is the property of *Mother Nature*.

In newspaper writing, some verbal phrases also appear far more commonly than you would find them elsewhere: *sweep through, be driven by, pack winds, strew with, flee on foot, choke with emotion, struggle to make sense, be on hand* and *deal with grief*. Then there are a few other odd clichés, such as *in the wake of, in the face of, from the ashes, outpouring of support*, and *shocked and saddened*. The simple presence of clichés such as these can help us to know that an article is taken from a newspaper, wherever we encounter it.

Doing the horizontal polka!

Euphemisms, derived from the Greek for sounding good, are pleasanter ways of talking about less than pleasant things. On a letter of reference, having *a relaxed attitude to work* may make you feel better than being called lazy; being *economical with the truth* sounds more pleasing than telling a bare-faced lie; and *collateral damage* is less offensive than killing innocent civilians. These are all examples of using euphemisms to obscure meaning, so that something unpleasant isn't clearly stated. Even more extreme are euphemisms that attempt to make something bad actually sound good. Downsizing simply obscures the meaning of making workers redundant, but *rightsizing* makes it sound like a good thing for a company to be doing.

Perhaps the most common use of euphemisms, however, is to avoid directly mentioning taboo subjects. Where do you go to urinate? *Toilet* originally meant a bag for clothes, but later became used as a euphemism for where you urinate (this is difficult to talk about, since all of the usual terms were originally euphemisms – lavatory, bathroom, washroom and so on). Now in the US *toilet* itself has become less than polite, so people ask where the *restroom* is, even when resting is the last thing they want to do.

The number of such replacement terms for most taboo subjects is astounding. Taboos commonly referred to by euphemisms include:

- ∞ death – *go the way of all flesh, push up daisies, put on the wooden overcoat.*

- ❧ urination – *feed the goldfish, answer the call of nature* and *go to see a man about a dog.*
- ❧ pregnancy, especially if it's unwanted – *be in the family way, have a bun in the oven* and *be eating for two.*
- ❧ menstruation – *have the monthly trouble, be closed for maintenance* and *ride the crimson wave.*
- ❧ male masturbation – *bash the candle, shake hands with the unemployed* and *be your own best friend.*
- ❧ sex – *have carnal knowledge, do the horizontal polka* and *make bacon.*

One Monty Python sketch contained 13 euphemisms for penis, all nicely sung along to a Noël Coward-style accompaniment. If you're wondering, the song includes *tadger*, *John Thomas* and *one-eyed trouser snake*. As you can see, many taboo-avoiding euphemisms are actually picturesque and amusing. My favourite is *worshipping the white porcelain god* as a substitution for vomiting.

Just in case you're feeling that everything sounds too nice, **dysphemisms** are the opposite of euphemisms. These are ways of being particularly offensive or disparaging when talking about something. Examples include the words *cripple*, *retard* and *moron* (the last two originally being euphemisms, but, like toilet, taking on pejorative connotations and becoming their opposite in effect).

One part in a processed tree carcass

Politically correct or PC language has been a major battlefield in the development of English since the early 1990s. Basically, PC language consists of words that have been altered to avoid offence based on race, gender, disability or anything else. So, using PC terms, a disabled person is called a *differently abled* person, and a prostitute is a *sex worker*. Avoiding offence is surely a good thing, and in some cases PC English offers a great improvement over more traditional expressions. For example, the word Eskimo is viewed by the people it refers to as disparaging, so *Inuit* or *Aleut* (depending on location) is preferable.

Other serious suggestions for PC alternatives to traditional terms are perhaps less suitable as they are only comprehensible to those in the know. Apparently, minorities should be called *emergent groups* and politically incorrect itself should be termed *appropriately inclusive*. There is also an issue of whether those referred to by PC terms actually want them to be used. Many blind people are proud of the word *blind* and prefer it to *visually disadvantaged*, some deaf people don't like being called *acoustically challenged*, and some dumb people find being called *non-verbal speaking* patronising. (Note that using these three PC terms would cause great difficulties in retaining the metre of the famous line from The Who song 'Pinball Wizard': 'That deaf, dumb and blind kid sure plays a mean pinball.')

As with so many good ideas, PC language can be taken too far. Some argue that it is an Orwellian attempt to shape people's ideas. Others simply view it as a joke. Indeed, the term politically correct is now probably used more often mockingly than seriously. The extremes of PC language (including, in some people's opinion, some of those terms above) have been parodied widely, with James Finn Garner's *Politically Correct Bedtime Stories* being a notable example. In the tale of 'Chicken Little', for instance, here is the satirical version of what happens after the eponymous heroine is hit on the head by an acorn:

> *Now, while Chicken Little had a small brain in the physical sense, she did use it to the best of her abilities. So when she screamed, 'The sky is falling, the sky is falling!' her conclusion was not wrong or stupid or silly, only logically under-enhanced.*

Parodies of PC language generally involve suggesting ludicrously extreme alternatives for inoffensive or only moderately distasteful words. Worst becomes *least best*, clumsy becomes *uniquely coordinated*, and ugly becomes *cosmetically different*. And a book could be called a *processed tree carcass* to highlight environmental issues.

Here are some more tongue-in-cheek PC terms. Can you match them to their traditional alternatives?

Living impaired	Beggar
Achieve a deficiency	Dead
Unaffiliated applicant for private-sector funding	Dirty old man
	Fail
Mobility-disadvantaged-unfriendly means of ascent	Ladder
Sexually focused cleanliness-impaired chronologically gifted individual	

The use of PC terms as replacements for potentially offensive normal English words is the most high-profile aspect of PC language. There is another application that involves what some might call excessive respect for all possible opinions. This is well illustrated by the following satire of a PC Christmas/New Year message (source unknown), which is regularly passed around the internet:

> *Please accept with no obligation, implied or implicit, my best wishes for an environmentally conscious, socially responsible, low-stress, non-addictive, gender-neutral celebration of the winter solstice holiday, practised within the most enjoyable traditions of the religious persuasion of your choice, or secular practices of your choice, with respect for the religious/secular persuasions and/or traditions of others, or their choice not to practise religious or secular traditions at all; and a fiscally successful, personally fulfilling, and medically uncomplicated recognition of the onset of the generally accepted calendar year 2006, but not without due respect for the calendars of choice of other cultures, and without regard to the race, creed, colour, age, physical ability, religious faith, choice of computer platform, or sexual preference of the wishees.*

God save the baked bean

Slang is ubiquitous. Even the most straitlaced speaker uses slang, albeit not the argot of modern-day ghettoes, but the vernacular of the ghettoes of 200 years ago or more that has now entered the everyday language (such as *bamboozle*, *fiasco* and *double-cross*). Despite such frequent shifts of slang into mainstream English, it is still often looked on with disapprobation; for example, in his *Devil's Dictionary* Ambrose Bierce defined it as 'the grunt of the human hog'. Nevertheless, slang is often creative and may even border on the poetic.

Slang is usually defined as informal non-standard use of words, and this definition points to the source of most of this kind of jargon. Although it occasionally involves the coining of words or the borrowing of foreign words, the most frequent way of creating slang is to give existing words new meanings. For example, the plethora of slang terms for the drug LSD includes *acid, animal, beast, blackbird, blue chairs, brown dots, California sunshine, coffee, contact lens, dental floss, flash, ghost, haze, mind detergent, pink panther, potato, sacrament, teddy bears, wedding bells* and, infamously, the title of a Beatles' song.

Such a vast array of terms for a single drug is due to the main reason for the existence of these colloquialisms. Although Eric Partridge in the 1930s identified 15 reasons for using slang (including the desire to be picturesque), the main purpose is to provide an in-group identity, usually for marginalised social groups. So drug users do not go around talking about their desire for lysergic acid diethylamide. Rather, they create new terms to refer to the substance to show that they are au fait and members of the social group of drug users.

Perhaps the best-known regional vernacular is **Cockney rhyming slang**. As the name suggests, this form of slang involves finding a word or phrase that rhymes with the target word, and using this rhyme instead. For instance, *baked bean* is the rhyming slang for queen (though I'm not aware of any attempts to make the British national anthem into 'God Save the Baked Bean'), *Adam and Eve* is believe, *apples and pears* is stairs, *brown bread* is dead, *dog and bone* is telephone, *frog and toad* is road, *jam jar* is car, *jam tart* is heart and *tea leaf* is thief. Knowing these, the following seemingly incomprehensible passage can actually start to make sense:

> *You'll never Adam and Eve what happened to me the other day. As I was walking down the frog and toad, I saw a tea leaf trying to steal a jam jar. Well, my jam tart was racing, so I rushed up the apples and pears and got on the dog and bone to the police, but the line was brown bread.*

Cockney rhyming slang has been used in the East End of London since the sixteenth century as a way of obscuring meaning, so that those not in the know cannot pass themselves off as Cockneys or follow what's said. While it's likely that, in common with most slang, rhymes were simply a way of identifying with a social group, it has been suggested that Cockney rhyming slang was originally a criminal argot designed to allow thieves to communicate without their victims understanding. Nowadays many of the phrases have become part of everyday British English, and often the people using them are unaware of their origins.

For example, the phrase *rabbit on* (as in she's always rabbiting on about her boyfriend, meaning she doesn't stop talking about him) is fairly common in British English. Here, the word *rabbit* comes from Cockney rhyming slang. The phrase *rabbit and pork* rhymes with talk and is shortened to simply *rabbit*. Other fairly common uses of rhyming slang in British English include *have a butcher's* meaning take a look (deriving from *butcher's hook*, rhyming with look), and *berk* meaning a person you dislike, which derives from a word rhyming with Berkshire hunt (given its origins, it's surprising how innocuous *berk* seems). These examples show that the most common form of rhyming slang involves finding a phrase that rhymes with the target word, and then using just the first half of the phrase as the slang term.

Children talk about making a raspberry (from *raspberry tart*, meaning fart) noise, albeit through their mouths; people are told 'Use your loaf' (from *loaf of bread*, meaning head) instead of being told to think; being informed that you have big jugs (from *jugs of beer*, meaning ear) may make you conscious of your ears (jugs is also slang for breasts, presumably because these represent jugs of milk to a baby); and people complain of having no bread (from *bread and honey*, meaning money). With a little more logic, even if chauvinistic, a wife can be called the trouble (from *trouble and strife*).

Even these examples are child's play compared to one particular piece of Cockney rhyming slang. *Plaster* is slang for arse. The reasoning goes as follows: plaster comes from Plaster of Paris, which rhymes with Aris, which comes from Aristotle, which rhymes with bottle, which comes from bottle and glass, which rhymes with arse.

Part IV
Meanings

All meanings, we know, depend on the key of interpretation.
George Eliot

The main purpose of language is to convey meanings. And it's amazing what strange and wondrous meanings can be transmitted through a single word in English. The sheer volume of words and the varied and intricate nuances that they can carry result in even native speakers needing to resort to dictionaries quite frequently. And of course, it's not only individual words that convey our meanings – how we put them together is often more important. The most interesting way in which words are combined is through metaphors, which allow us easily to express previously unthought-of meanings, some of which will be revealed in this section.

Ostrobogulous words

E nglish is full of **strange and wondrous words**, and in this chapter we look at some of the strangest and most wondrous.

One way in which English words are wondrous is their pronunciation. Some just sound attractive. This may be because of the way letters and sounds are repeated through a word, as in *zenzizenzizenzic* (meaning the eighth power of a number) and *syzygy* (meaning a conjunction of the moon and the sun). Other words sound attractive because of the rhythmic pattern they create when spoken, for instance *ostrobogulous* (meaning unusual) and *tatterdemalion* (meaning a ragamuffin, itself an attractive word). Finally, there are words that are reminiscent of more familiar terms but with a twist, like *wabbit* (meaning unwell) and *mugwump* (meaning a fence-sitter).

Another way in which words are wondrous is their meanings. Some of the strangest concepts can be expressed using a single English word. For example, the act of employing your fingers to help you count is called *dactylonomy*; if you urinate backwards you are *retromingent*; and if you call two people *unasinous*, you mean that they are equally stupid. The strangest single word that I'm aware of is *spanghew*, which apparently means to throw a frog into the air, a concept so weird that you wonder why anyone would ever feel the need to coin a word for it.

These wondrous meanings of obscure words led to the creation of a British television programme called *Call My Bluff*. In this programme, each team of three contestants is given an obscure word with an unusual meaning, plus two additional false senses for the same word. Poker faced, the team proposes the three definitions to the opposing team, whose task it is to guess which description is true.

For the following words with strange meanings, two of the definitions are false. Can you call my bluff and identify the true sense?

Antinomian
1 Referring to the belief that faith in Christ frees you from following legal and moral obligations.
2 Derived from the name of the metal antimony and meaning wearing only white clothes.
3 Refusing ever to use a name; permanently anonymous.

Cynanthropy
1 A passionate dislike of the colour blue.
2 A form of madness in which the sufferer believes that he or she is a dog.
3 The paranoid belief that people around you are robots.

Psychopomp
1 A love for using complex ecclesiastical paraphernalia, often used as a criticism of Catholicism.
2 Excessive self-belief resulting in believing that every-one likes you, even when evidence is to the contrary.
3 A guide to heaven and hell for the dead.

Ultracrepidarian
1 Making pronouncements on topics about which you know nothing.
2 Constantly taking arguments to extremes.
3 Having a face that is very frightening.

Not all unusual words have incredibly obscure meanings that we will probably never use. A few concern everyday things that we don't ever talk about, perhaps partly because we don't know the terms for them. The squiggles and lines you see floating around when you close your eyes are called *muscae volitantes*, for instance, and the stretching that accompanies a yawn is *pandiculation*. Although little known, these words have a lot more potential usefulness than terms like *antinomian* (referring to the belief that faith in Christ frees you from following legal and moral obligations), *cynanthropy* (a form of madness in which the sufferer believes that he or she is a dog), *psychopomp* (a guide to heaven and hell for the dead) and *ultracrepidarian* (making pronouncements on topics about which you know nothing).

What is a loquacious agnostic?

Dictionaries are supposed to contain all the most useful words in a language. Generally, this means that they include nearly all the non-technical terms you're likely to come across in everyday life. Some of the words in a dictionary, however, are more likely to be referred to than others. Most people are not likely to look up the terms they already know. For example, would you consult a dictionary for the word *the*?

On the other hand, words that are very rare are also less likely to be looked up, since people do not encounter them very often. I'm willing to bet quite a lot that you have never delved into a dictionary for the word *amphisbaena*, since you are unlikely to have come across it before (it means a lizard with a head at both ends).

The words that are most frequently looked up are those that are at the edge of people's knowledge – they're terms that you feel you should know but that you're not really certain about. We can gain some grasp of their nature by examining the words that online dictionaries are most commonly consulted for. The most frequently looked-up word in one survey was *anomaly*, and the rest of the top 10 were:

ethereal	fascist
loquacious	sycophant
empathy	facetious
agnostic	capricious
protocol	

Other surveys of the use of online dictionaries tend to high-light fashions in words – for instance, the most frequently looked up word in 2004 was *blog* – rather than general uncertainties about how to say what we mean.

She slept like a hot knife through butter

Metaphors are simply ways of comparing one thing to another. Strictly, we should distinguish between metaphors where the comparison is direct (e.g. *He is a bear*) and similes, which include words indicating that a comparison is being made (e.g. *He is like a bear*). For the sake of simplicity here, I'll lump them all together as metaphors.

People use metaphors for a variety of reasons. Evocative metaphors can add spice (itself a metaphor) and interest to our words. They can grab attention, conjure up deeper levels of insight, and allow us to talk about complex or new concepts in accessible ways. Truly stimulating metaphors that make us pause and think can be found in any good novel. Often they are a single phrase, such as Shakespeare's *Cowards whose hearts are all as false as stairs of sand*, but a metaphor can also provide the underpinnings of a whole argument. Quoting Shakespeare again:

> *There is a tide in the affairs of men,*
> *Which, taken at the flood, leads on to fortune;*
> *Omitted, all the voyage of their life*
> *Is bound in shallows and in miseries.*
> *On such a full sea are we now afloat;*
> *And we must take the current when it serves,*
> *Or lose our ventures.*

On the downside, many metaphors have become clichés, and they can also be employed as a way out of trying to express thoughts exactly. Not everyone can use metaphors as evocatively as Shakespeare, and they can be bland and boring. For instance, what does *like a fish* add to the meaning of *He swam through the sea like a fish?*

An interesting way of avoiding clichés and creating new ideas is to mix and match different bland metaphors. We all know that a thing can *soar through the air like a bird* and that the same thing may *sink through water like a stone.* But how about something *soaring through the air like a stone* or *sinking through water like a bird?* What about a person *sleeping like clockwork* or *like a hot knife through butter*, instead of *like a baby?* While nowhere near Shakespeare, such combinations do at least conjure up new images.

The mixing of metaphors above is intentional, but amusing mistakes often result from unintentional **mixed metaphors**, where metaphors are combined in one sentence with sometimes ludicrous consequences. Some inappropriate mixed metaphors occur when two or more different metaphors are used consecutively. For example, Sir Boyle Roche, an eighteenth-century Irish MP, is reputed to have said: *I smell a rat. I see him forming in the air and darkening the sky; but I'll nip him in the bud.* Even more amusing are instances where the mixed metaphors are in the same clause and logically inconsistent, such as *He's trying to gain a foothold in the public eye* or *You'll get into hot water skating on thin ice.*

A second type of mixed metaphor results from confusion between similar metaphors. For example, *hitting the nail on the head* and *hitting the jackpot* both involve hitting and have similar meanings. A little slip of the tongue can result in *She hit the nail on the jackpot.*

Although most of us are familiar with metaphors from our literature classes at school or become aware of using such devices when we make a right hash of them, our use is normally unconscious. In writing this chapter, when talking about *lumping together* metaphors and similes and *conjuring up* insights, I did not intentionally decide to use metaphors. Rather, such figures of speech underlie much everyday language and so are difficult to avoid. Many idioms are based on metaphors, such as *spilling the beans* and *paying through the nose* (which would be rather disgusting if literal), and widely accepted phrases such as Abraham Lincoln's *rebirth of the nation* are also metaphorical.

In fact, the ubiquity of metaphors has led linguists to the conclusion that much of our thinking is organised along metaphorical lines. So we may understand anger as being equivalent to heat, and talk about *boiling with rage*, *simmering* or *burning with anger* and even *venting anger* (to release the pressure caused by the build-up of heat). Similarly, while we may consciously use a proverb like *Time is money*, we don't normally consider the financial implications of *spending time*, *investing time*, *buying time* or things *costing time*.

As well as guiding our thinking, metaphors may actually dictate the direction of science. Paul Davies, a renowned physicist, has argued that the metaphor of the most esteemed technology of the day has driven physics. Thus, in ancient Greece where musical instruments were the pinnacle of technology, the universe was seen in terms of numbers and harmony; the wonders of clock technology led to the clockwork universe of Isaac Newton; this was replaced in the steam engine-dominated nineteenth century with a universe where entropy became paramount; and in the current computer age, physicists study the universe as if it were made up of information.

The real importance of metaphors therefore lies in how they pervade our language use and even our thinking.

Part V

Peculiarities

All that is really necessary for survival of the fittest, it seems, is an interest in life, good, bad, or peculiar.

Grace Paley

Although some of the peculiarities of English are so obscure that arcane technical terms for strange figures of speech have been coined to describe them, others are part of our everyday language. In a language as curious as English, even things as prosaic as forming plurals, the alphabet, vowels and consecutive pairs of letters can be marvellously odd. Associated with the nursery are reduplicated words, and there are also the notoriously strange collective nouns. So let's start examining the intriguing peculiarities of English

This chapter is sound – all sound

The pun on the word *sound* in the title of this chapter is adapted from a famous quotation by Benjamin Franklin: *Your argument is sound, nothing but sound.* Such clever use of a word may seem to be an isolated instance of genius, but there is in fact a technical term for this type of pun. It's called **antanaclasis**, defined as repeating a word with a changed meaning in the second use. Other examples include Vince Lombardi's *If you aren't fired with enthusiasm, you will be fired with enthusiasm* and the British Airways advert, *Our frequent fliers can frequent other fliers.*

Antanaclasis is just one of a surprising range of obscure, and eminently forgettable, technical terms for strange figures of speech, applying both to individual words and whole sentences. While the terms themselves may be off-putting, some of the figures of speech are fascinating.

For individual words, the exactness of the technical terms is daunting. For instance, if you insert an additional sound or syllable into the middle of a word (as in *um-buh-rella*) it's called **epenthesis**, whereas if you introduce a whole word (e.g. *any-old-how* and *guaran-goddamn-tee*) it's called **tmesis**.

Here are a few more technical terms for unusual adaptations of individual words, with definitions and examples from Shakespeare:

- ∞ **Aphaeresis**: omitting a letter or syllable at the beginning of a word – Who should *'scape* whipping.
- ∞ **Apocope**: omitting a letter or syllable at the end of a word – When I *ope* my lips let no dog bark.

- ∞ **Prosthesis**: adding an extra syllable to the start of a word – All alone, I *beweep* my outcast state.
- ∞ **Syncope**: omitting letters or sounds in the middle of a word – I have but with a cursorary eye *o'erglanc'd* the articles.

From these examples it may seem that these figures of speech are restricted to highfalutin literature, but we use instances in everyday speech. When we say *street cred* (not credibility) or talk about the *Fab Four* (instead of fabulous), we are employing apocope. Two of the three Rs in education (*Riting* and *Rithmetic*) exhibit aphaeresis, and syncope can be found in *fo'c's'le*.

While the single-word figures of speech are interesting, it's those involving whole sentences that are really clever, as we saw with antanaclasis. The names for these figures of speech are often intimidating, but they are worth pondering for a moment.

To start with there's **catachresis**, which means an intentional flagrant violation of normal rules of language. This includes deliberately using words strangely and mixing metaphors. From Shakespeare again, we have *To take arms against a sea of troubles* (though the results of fighting a sea are unclear) and *'Tis deepest winter in Lord Timon's purse*, which is a strikingly unusual, if literally inappropriate metaphor. An interesting subcategory of catachresis is **synaesthesia** or mixing the senses, as in Shakespeare's *Look with thine ears*.

Another particularly striking figure of speech is **hyperbaton**, or intentionally using a strange word order. From Shakespeare we have *Constant you are, but yet a woman* (instead of you are constant), but there are plenty of more recent examples. At the other end of the cultural spectrum is

Yoda, who in *Attack of the Clones* says *Grave danger you are in*. More amusingly Winston Churchill, on being told that he should never end a sentence with a preposition, is often attributed as noting, *This is the sort of arrant pedantry up with which I will not put*. It's amazing how far it is possible to push English word order while still retaining comprehensibility. The master of this is probably the poet e e cummings (his use of capital letters is an instance of catachresis). One example of his work is *Me up at does out of the floor quietly Stare a poisoned mouse*.

Another neat figure of speech is **antimetabole**, which is a reversed repetition, as in the Shakespearean *Fair is foul, and foul is fair*. Several other well-known sayings are examples: *When the going gets tough, the tough get going,* and John F Kennedy's *Ask not what your country can do for you; ask what you can do for your country*.

A final intriguing figure of speech is **zeugma**. This means using a single verb with two objects, where each object requires a different meaning of the verb. That sounds complex, but a few sentences should illustrate what a zeugma involves. The best-known example is probably *He took his hat and his leave*; Alexander Pope wrote *losing her heart or her necklace at the ball*; and from the linguist Alan Cruse comes *John and his driver's license expired on Tuesday*.

Two dog-dog

Different languages form **plurals** in different ways. Some languages, such as Thai, don't differentiate between singular and plural nouns, so that you talk about *one dog* and *two dog*. Others make the logical step of simply using a noun twice to indicate a plural. So in Indonesian, you could have *two dog-dog*. Fortunately these languages stop at a single repetition of the noun; otherwise you'd have to talk about the six wife-wife-wife-wife-wife-wife of Henry VIII, and the 'Twelve Days of Christmas' would take forever to sing.

Most European languages, on the other hand, add a marker at the end of the noun to show a plural. In the case of English, of course, this marker is usually an *s*. It's not quite that simple, however (nothing is ever simple with English). While in writing we may just add an *s* to the end of a word to show a plural, there are three ways in which this plural ending can be pronounced. Try saying the following:

- backs
- bags
- badges

Depending on the preceding sound, the extra *s* can be pronounced as 's', 'z' or 'iz'.

Even then, English being English, there are lots of exceptions. Adding *es* to the end of words is almost as common as adding just *s*. So we get *wishes* not *wishs* and, fortunately, *kisses* not *kisss*. Generally, whether to add *s* or *es* to the end of a noun to make a plural depends on the final letter or sound. Words ending in *-ch*, *-sh*, *-ss* and *-zz* always add *es*.

Well, nearly always. Saying 'always' when describing English is very dangerous – there are always exceptions (and maybe there are exceptions to whether there are exceptions). For instance, the plural of *loch* (ending in *-ch*, but without the usual *-ch* sound) is *lochs*, not *loches*.

Of course, since we're dealing with English, the *s* or *es* endings must be even more complex than they at first appear, and this is the case for words ending in *-o*. Some of these words make a plural by adding just *s* (*kilos*, *memos*), some by adding *es* (*heroes*, *potatoes*), and some can do both (*mosquitos* or *mosquitoes*, *volcanos* or *volcanoes*). Perhaps it's not surprising that poor Dan Quayle (the Vice President under George Bush) infamously misspelt *potatoes* as *potatos*. *

Then there are other letters at or near the ends of words that need their own rules. One of them is *-f*, which often (but not always) turns into *-ves* in a plural. So we have *elves*, *knives* and *wolves*. A couple of words ending in *-f*, however, can either add *s* or change to *-ves* (*roofs* or *rooves* and *dwarfs* or *dwarves*), the choice seeming to depend on personal preference.

While the *s* plural form predominates in English, there are a surprising number of other possible ways of making plurals. Most of these unusual forms exist because the words were borrowed (and presumably not returned) from other languages. In addition to borrowing the words themselves, the foreign plural forms were also retained.

While not strictly foreign words, a few words from Old English still retain the original plural ending *en*. Most Old English words have changed to taking the plural *s* (now it is *names*, not *namen*), but we still talk about *oxen*, *children* and *brethren*.

* No - potato as potatoe.

There are a few even weirder plurals coming from Old and Middle English. There are three words that make plurals by changing two vowels, three words that form plurals by changing all except their first and last letters, a six-letter word that makes a plural by changing all except the first two letters, and even an old-fashioned plural that has no letters in common with its singular form. Can you think of what they are?

Many words borrowed from Latin retain the original plural forms. Some add *e* to words ending in -*a* (*algae, formulae, vertebrae*), others change -*us* to -*i* (*cacti, fungi, stimuli*) and still others change -*um* to -*a* (*data, media, strata*). Then there are Latin words ending in both -*ix* and -*ex* that have an -*ices* ending in the plural (*cervices, matrices, apices, vortices*), and a Latin word ending in -*us* may change to -*ora* (*corpora*) or -*era* (*genera*) in the plural.

There are similar irregular plurals for words borrowed from Greek. Some words ending in -*is* change to -*es* (*analyses, crises, oases*), others ending in -*on* change to -*a* (*criteria, phenomena*), and a couple of words add -*ta* to make a plural (*schemata, stomata*). Other lending languages where the original plural forms are retained are Italian (-*o* changing to -*i* in musical terms such as *libretti* and *virtuosi*) and Hebrew (adding an -*im*, as in *cherubim* and *kibbutzim*).

Although these plurals may seem strange, the oddest of all, as we saw in the quiz, originate in Old English. Plurals like *feet, geese, teeth, lice, mice* and *men* (and *women*) all come from laziness in speaking. It's easier to say *mice* than *mouses*. If you try saying *mouses* over and over again very quickly, you'll find that the middle vowel changes to an *i*, the so-called i-mutation. The weirdest plural of all that has no letters in common with its singular form also comes from Old English. The Old English for cow was *cy*, and this word developed in two separate directions, one becoming the *cow* and *cows* we are familiar with and the other, the original plural using an Old English *-en* form, changing into the old-fashioned word *kine*. So you could talk about one cow and two kine if you wanted to. The last of the strange plurals, the six-letter word in the quiz, exists because two different words with similar meanings were borrowed from Old French, one to indicate the singular – *person* – and one to denote the plural – *people*.

Given the large number of strange plurals in English, it should come as no surprise that several words have more than one possible plural form. Most commonly, the two forms are the plural deriving from the original source language (e.g. *media* is the plural of *medium*) and, if the word has become well integrated into English, the standard English plural (e.g. *mediums*). For some words with two meanings, the different senses take different plurals. So for *medium*, when talking about things like radio and television the plural is *media*, but for people who act as spiritual connections to the afterlife we would be more likely to use *mediums*. Similarly, at the back of books we find *appendices*, but a doctor may perform operations to remove *appendixes*.

The two champions for variations in plurals are *octopus* and *rhinoceros*. The two most obvious plurals of octopus are *octopuses* and (incorrectly since the root is Greek, not Latin) *octopi*. The proper Greek plural is *octopodes* – so three possible plurals for octopus. Similarly for rhinoceros, we have *rhinoceroses*, *rhinoceri* (incorrectly), *rhinoceros* (presumably pronounced differently from the singular) and (an obsolete but correct form) *rhinocerotes*. In fact, rhinoceros is the English word with the most possible plural forms: four in all.

Even more confusingly, one word may be the plural form of two different singular words. So *bases* means more than one of both *base* and *basis*, and *ellipses* can refer to both *ellipse* and *ellipsis*. The winner in this category is *axes*, which is the plural of *ax*, *axe* and *axis*.

Obviously, not all English words have such complex plurals. Indeed, quite a few make no change from singular to plural (just like Thai), so we have one *sheep* and two *sheep*. For others, like *rendezvous*, the spellings of the singular and plural are the same, but the pronunciations are different.

Other words that don't change from singular to plural include *trousers* and *scissors*. This category encompasses various clothes (*braces*, *dungarees*, *jeans*, *overalls*, *pants* and *shorts*), things comprising two parts (*pliers*, *secateurs* and *shears*) and a few other odd words (*agenda*, *alms*, *eaves*, *ides* and *marginalia*). These words are always plural and don't have a singular form, so it isn't really the case that they don't change form for a plural. They are different in nature to the animals (*deer* and lots of fish – *cod*, *perch*, *tuna*, *salmon*, *trout* and *halibut*, among others), traditionally plural words (*barracks*, *crossroads*, *gallows*, *headquarters*, *means*, *series* and *species*) and French words (*chassis*, *corps*, *faux pas* and *précis*), where the singular and plural forms, at least in written language, really are the same.

At this point it may seem that there aren't too many words left to take the regular s plural ending, but of course there are. Even with these words, there is a twist in the tale. There are three plural words that do the opposite of most words – add an s to them and they become singular. *Cares* becomes *caress*, *princes* becomes *princess*, and *timelines* becomes *timeliness*. This does go to show that nothing is simple in English.

The upside-down ox

There are two main types of writing. One is where the written symbols generally stand for whole words, as in Chinese. The other is the **alphabet**, where the symbols (or letters) represent sounds and need to be combined to make words. Although it is the subject of some controversy, the first alphabet was probably created by the Phoenicians in the east Mediterranean around 1600 BCE (although a recent Egyptian discovery may date to about 1800 BCE). The Phoenician alphabet contained only consonants, and it was the Greeks around 800 BCE who added vowels to make an alphabet akin to those we are familiar with now.

The letters of the alphabet were originally pictograms, or stylised pictures of familiar objects. A, for example, is derived from a portrayal of an ox. Over the years it has been turned upside-down, so if you draw an upside-down letter A and use a little imagination, you can see an ox's face with the legs of the A representing the horns.

Here are some other pairings of letters and pictograms. Which letters were derived from which pictograms?

B	whip
H	eye
L	fence
M	house
O	water

B comes from house – imagine a narrow two-storey building. H is a fence – put lots of Hs together. L is a long thin whip, M is the ripples of water, and O is a round eye.

Obviously, the letters in the alphabet don't appear with the same frequency. For example, *e* is far more common than *z* – a fact reflected in the letter scores in a Scrabble® set. In fact, *e* is the most common letter in English. In most texts *e* accounts for about one-eighth of the letters, and about two-thirds of English words contain *e*.

The full list of letter frequencies in English is *etaoinshrdlucmfgypwbvkxjqz*. This is, in fact, the sequence of the letters used in linotype typesetting machines. The exact order of **frequencies of letters**, however, depends on the source of the data you're counting. For example, if we take the *Book of Psalms* in the King James Bible, the sequence is *ethoaisnrldmufygwcpbvkjqxz*. The series can be very different in other languages. For example, the 12 most frequent letters in French are *esaitnrulodm*, while in Welsh they are *ayndreiloghw*.

The overriding frequency of the letter *e* in English and other languages has led some surely demented authors to produce what are called **lipograms**. These are books in which one letter is purposefully left out completely. So in 1939 Ernest Vincent Wright published a 50,000-word novel entitled *Gadsby*, which did not contain the letter *e*. The first sentence of the book is as follows.

> *If youth, throughout all history, had had a champion to stand up for it; to show a doubting world that a child can think; and, possibly, do it practically, you wouldn't constantly run across fools today who claim that 'a child don't know anything'.*

Similarly, in 1969 George Perec wrote a 20-page French novella entitled *La Disparition*, also omitting the letter *e*. Amazingly, this work was translated into English as *A Void* by

Gilbert Adair in 1995, still without an *e*. This translation starts

> Noon rings out. A wasp, making an ominous sound, a
> sound akin to a klaxon or a tocsin, flits about.

A few words in English have interesting alphabetical characteristics, and we might call these **alphabet words**. For example, the letters of both *beefily* and *billowy* are in alphabetical order, although the double letters are suspect. With no repeated letters, the six-letter words *abhors* and *chimps* are probably the longest alphabet words in English. Similarly, there are several English words with the letters in reverse alphabetical order. Allowing double letters, *spoonfeed* is the longest.

Another alphabetical characteristic of words concerns those with letters from only half the alphabet. For example, the 12-letter words *fickleheaded* and *fiddledeedee* contain letters from the first half of the alphabet only (A–M), while the 11-letter word *nonsupports* is made up of letters from the second half of the alphabet (N–Z).

There are also words that contain alphabetical sequences of letters. For instance, *abcoulomb* (a unit of electric charge) contains the sequence *abc*. There are two four-letter series that can appear in English words: *mnop* and *rstu*. The words containing *mnop* are generally obscure, such as *gymnophobia* and *somnopathy*. More familiar are words including *rstu*, such as *overstudious*, *superstud* and *understudy*.

The iouae sang euouae

How many **vowels** are there in English? The easy answer is five, although you might guess six (or, being particularly clever, five and a half) if you include the semi-vowel *y*. These numbers refer to written vowels only. The number of spoken vowel sounds in English is much higher, with numbers ranging from 20 to 40 depending on how they're counted. This massive difference between the numbers of written and spoken vowels is one of the main reasons for the confusion between English spelling and pronunciation.

Focusing on written vowels (and not including *y*), English has many interesting features. One is that several words don't include vowels. The most familiar of these is probably the seven-letter *rhythms*, although there's also an obscure twelve-letter word *twyndyllyngs* (meaning twins). Similarly, some surprisingly long words manage with only one letter that is a vowel, the nine-letter *strengths* being a good example.

On the other hand, vowels predominate in other words. There is supposed to be an English word written *euouae* (no idea of the pronunciation but apparently it's a guideline for how to sing a Gregorian chant), which consists only of vowels. As with most record-breaking words, this is excessively obscure. More familiar, but with only five consecutive vowels, are *queueing* and *cooeeing*. If you're happy with unfamiliarity and allow for place names, the record for consecutive vowels goes to several places in North Africa, such as *Ijouaououene* in Morocco and *Aguinaouiaoui* in Mali, each with eight consecutive vowels.

In words with long vowel clusters, some of the vowels inevitably appear more than once. Other English words contain all five vowels only once each. Going back to complete obscurity, *iouae* is a genus of fossil sponges (clearly not a very useful word for everyday conversation) and *eunoia* means a normal state of mind.

Amid a plethora of opaque words, there are a couple of somewhat more familiar seven-letter words that contain all five vowels once. Can you think of them?

In addition to these two words, *sequoia* and *miaoued*, there is *caesious*, again abstruse and describing the colour of lavender, which is the shortest English word with all five vowels in alphabetical order, while the even shorter and, if possible, more recondite *suoidea* (it's a fossil pig) has the vowels in reverse alphabetical order. Other more common words with these characteristics are *facetious*, *abstemious*, *subcontinental* and *uncomplimentary*. And there's also a word with each of the five vowels appearing twice: *ultrarevolutionaries*.

Then again, some fairly long English words rely on only one repeated vowel. For example, the obscure *monophthongs* (an appropriate word since it means single vowel sounds) is the longest word that only uses *o* as a vowel. (*Chrononhotonthologos* appears under 'blusterer' in *Roget's Thesaurus*, but is derived from a proper name.) Similarly, for *i* there are *disinhibiting* and *primitivistic*, and for *a* we have *handcraftsman*. Words like *strengthlessnesses*, *dumbstruck* and *untruthful* also use only one vowel.

There are several long English words that alternate vowels and consonants. The longest is probably *parasitological*, while *unimaginative* comes close. Again allowing for place names, the *United Arab Emirates* probably holds the record.

Finally, some words rely more on consonants than vowels, but other words have long stretches of consonants with no vowels in sight. So *sightscreen* and *catchphrase* both have six consecutive consonants.

Brrrr! Shhhh!

All languages (perhaps with the exception of the whistling language of shepherds on the Canary Islands) contain vowels and consonants. As we have already seen, some alphabets, especially ancient ones, consist only of consonants. Most modern alphabets, however, incorporate both vowels and consonants, and these appear in different patterns depending on the language. At one extreme is Japanese, which has a tendency to alternate vowels and consonants – think of *Toyota* and *Kawasaki*. At the other extreme is Polish, which can contain long sequences of consonants that seem unpronounceable to English speakers, such as the towns *Bydgoszcz* and *Walbrzych*.

English falls somewhere in the middle, with alternating vowels and consonants and pairs of vowels and consonants both frequent. Generally the consecutive letters in English are different, but certain letters often appear as pairs. For example, *appear* has a pair of *p*s. The most commonly occurring pairs of letters in English are, in order, *ss*, *ee* and *tt*.

It is in fact possible to come up with 26 words each incorporating a consecutive pair for all of the letters of the alphabet. Some of these, such as *avijja*, *huqqa*, *waxxenn* (for *x*) and *cubbyyew* (for *y*), are very obscure. For other letters a vast range of words contain pairs: *bubble*, *accent*, *odd*, *see*, *off*, *egg*, *ill*, *simmer*, *sinner*, *too*, *appear*, *err*, *ass*, *sitter* and *buzz*.

The interesting letters are those for which there are only a few words, albeit relatively familiar, which contain a pair of letters. Can you think of words including *aa*, *hh*, *ii*, *kk*, *uu*, *vv* and *ww*?

While **double letters** appear in words like *aardvark*, *withhold*, *beachhead*, *skiing*, *bookkeeper*, *vacuum*, *continuum*, *savvy* and *glowworm*, and one of these can even be adapted to give four pairs of double letters in a row (*subbookkeeper*), rather more rare are **triple letters**. They do exist for some of the letters where pairs are relatively common. For *e*, if we start with words ending in a double *e*, like *wee*, *free* and *agree*, and then add a suffix such as *-er* or *-est*, we end up with *weeer*, *freeest* and the person who agrees, the *agreeer*. Similarly for *l*, we can add the suffix *-less* to words ending in a double *l*, giving *gill-less*, *frillless* and a *mollless* gangster. Lastly for *s*, the suffix *-ship* gives us *princessship* and *governessship*. Most of these words with triple letters are dubious, but one indubitable triple letter is in the Scottish county *Rossshire*.

It is even possible for some letters to appear in a quadruple sequence. Most commonly this is in exaggerated exclamations like *brrrr* and *shhhh*, or in obsolete words like *esssse*, meaning ashes. Perhaps more familiarly, the famously long name of a town in Wales, *Llanfairpwllgwyngogerychwyrndrobwllllantysiliogogogoch*, contains four consecutive *l*s (although these would only be counted as a pair of *ll*s in Welsh). Less believable, if the person who agrees is the agreeer, does that mean that the person who is agreed with is the *agreeee*?

Although not strictly double or triple letters, a nice variant is consecutive dotted letters. The record is held by a company in northern Canada called *Katujjijiit Development Corporation*, while *Beijing* and *Fiji* have three dotted letters in a row.

Finally, in contrast to all the repetitions of letters, long words in which no letter appears more than once are surprisingly rare in English. The record holders are 15-letter words such as *uncopyrightable*, *dermatoglyphics* and *misconjugatedly*.

A tip-top higgledy-piggledy hodge-podge

For some reason English speakers seem to have a passion for **reduplicated words**, which come as two similar-sounding halves. From an early age when we might hear of a *teeny-weeny tootsy-wootsy* on a *piggy-wiggy* through our *namby-pamby* and *lardy-dardy* days until we are a *fuddy-duddy*, we use a *higgledy-piggledy hodge-podge* of reduplicated words *willy-nilly*.

There are probably around 100 of these reduplicated words, and they have a surprisingly august history. Shakespeare wrote of *skimble-skamble* stuff and no *tiddle-taddle* or *pibble-pabble*, and the pop song 'Itsy Bitsy Teeny Weeny Yellow Polka Dot Bikini' reached number one in the charts, although reduplicated words still sound childish.

Reduplicated words can be made in two ways. First, the initial consonant is changed in the second half of the word, as in *hurdy-gurdy* and *razzle-dazzle*. Second, the vowel is altered in the second part, such as *tip-top* and *zig-zag*.

In addition to reduplicated words like *see-saw, walkie-talkie, pow-wow, super-duper* and *pell-mell*, another English usage that comes in two halves consists of pairs of words that make set phrases. Problems can come *thick and fast* in the *cut and thrust* of modern business.

Many of these paired words have legal roots. Two words are used rather than one to ensure that too narrow an interpretation of a legal document is not taken. So a *will and testament* can be *null and void*. A second source is the *Book of Common Prayer*, which formed the basis of the religious practices of many English speakers for hundreds of years. In the prayer book believers are asked to *acknowledge and confess sins and wickedness*, among a host of other paired words.

From these roots we try to pick up the *bits and pieces*, put our *heart and soul* into doing our best by *all ways and means*, until, *lo and behold*, we are improving by *leaps and bounds*. In these phrases the two words have pretty much the same meaning, making you wonder why the second half is needed.

In other paired words, although the two words still have similar meanings, one of these may not be so clear. Rack in *rack and ruin* means destruction, and hue in *hue and cry* means outcry. In *spick and span*, the spick is a nail (like spike) and span is an abbreviation of *span new*, meaning very new. Flotsam is floating wreckage, while jetsam is wreckage washed ashore, so *flotsam and jetsam* means all of the things lost overboard or surviving a shipwreck.

A collective of nouns

Amid the myriad peculiarities of English, few aspects are more peculiar than **collective nouns**. These are words meaning 'group', but which word you use depends on what you are grouping. So we have a *flock of birds* but a *herd of deer*. Other familiar collective nouns are especially strange on reflection. We talk about a *pride of lions* or a *school of fish*, but are lions noticeably proud creatures or fish particularly studious?

The real beauty of collective nouns lies in those that are less familiar. In addition to *flocks of birds*, we also have *flocks of camels*. *Crows* are grouped into *murders*, and we get an *unkindness of ravens* and a *storytelling of rooks*. Matters become even stranger when we talk of *penguins* living in *rookeries*. Amazingly, there are collective nouns for creatures that are not well known: a *sedge of bitterns*, a *chain of bobolinks* and a *trip of dotterel*.

While there seems to be little reason for many of the collective nouns, for others there's a delightful logic linking the noun and the animal. *Hedgehogs* are grouped into *prickles* and *foxes* into *skulks*, and we have an *ambush of tigers* and a *shrewdness of apes*.

Can you match the following animals with the appropriate collective nouns?

Cats	Ostentation
Ducks	Bloat
Gnus	Crash
Hippopotami	Pounce
Peacocks	Paddling
Rhinoceroses	Implausibility

All the weird and wonderful phrases have led to some witty suggestions for new collective nouns. In fact, it's not really clear whether the collective nouns for animals in the quiz are really words with a long history of use as collective nouns or just recent jocular inventions. After all, a *pounce of cats*, a *paddling of ducks*, an *implausibility of gnus*, a *bloat of hippopotami*, an *ostentation of peacocks* and a *crash of rhinoceroses* are all amusing combinations.

Collective nouns don't only apply to animals. There are also specific collective nouns for some occupations and objects. We say a *bevy of beauties*, a *coven of witches* and a *congregation of worshippers*. We also talk about a *range of mountains*, a *fleet of ships* (no matter how slow they are) and a *flight of stairs* (even when they don't fly). Many witticisms also exist for people: a *ponder of philosophers*, an *exaggeration of fishermen*, a *revelation of flashers*, an *expectation of heirs*, a *balance of accountants* and an *absence of waiters*. In addition there are some neat puns, such as a *heard of noisy musicians*, a *hoard of misers* and a *whored of prostitutes*, as well as the groan-inducing a *virtue of patients*.

Part VI

Illogicalities

Life forms illogical patterns. It is haphazard and full of beauties which I try to catch as they fly by, for who knows whether any of them will ever return?

Margot Fonteyn

L anguages are created by people and, since people are often illogical, most languages contain elements of illogicality. If we could rank languages on how illogical they are, English would probably come in at number one. After all, this is a language where ordinary sentences are often ambiguous or even self-contradictory.

Illogicalities in English don't even need the comfortable length of a sentence to become apparent. Just two words together is enough to make illogical oxymorons, while other pairs of words form redundant pleonasms. And then there are the infamous double negatives – a long-standing bone of contention for logicians. With so many different ways to be illogical in English, it's a wonder we can understand one another at all.

Squad helps dog bite victim

Some classic **illogicalities** have been celebrated by many authors. For example, if we say one *mouse* and two *mice*, why don't we say one *house* and two *hice*? And with one *foot* and two *feet*, why not one *boot* and two *beet*? If teachers *teach*, why don't fingers *fing*? Why does your nose *run* but your feet *smell*? If you get *olive oil* from olives, where does *baby oil* come from? And if you get a *beer belly* from drinking beer, how do you get a *pot belly*?

Another comical aspect concerns what happens when you take all sentences literally. We say *She has a temperature*, but surely everything in the universe has a temperature? And what ridiculous situations could ensue if the following signs were taken literally?

- Dogs must be carried on the escalator.
- Any person not putting litter in this basket will be fined.
- White shirts only should be worn.

Ambiguities abound in English, partly because of the enormous number of words with at least two distinct meanings. When we hear *He went to the bank*, we need to know the context to know which sense of bank is intended and so whether he went to a river or a financial institution.

More interesting and amusing than word-based or lexical ambiguities are sentence ambiguities. For example, in the sentence *Children make great dinners*, are the children cooks or food?

These sentence-level ambiguities are probably most common in newspaper headlines, where sparse wording makes misinterpretations more likely. Here are my ten favourite ambiguous headlines – and yes, they are all real.

- Dealers to hear car talk at noon
- New vaccine may contain rabies
- Juvenile court to try shooting defendant
- Grandmother of eight makes hole in one
- Red tape holds up new bridge
- Complaints about NBA referees growing ugly
- Man minus ear waives hearing
- Miners refuse to work after death
- Infertility unlikely to be passed on
- Squad helps dog bite victim

Headlines such as these make us stop and think twice, as we realise that two interpretations are possible. Another type of sentence that forces us to think twice, but in this case as we search for a possible interpretation, is the **garden path sentence** (so called because the first part of the sentence leads us up the garden path by making us expect something that doesn't happen). For instance, *The cotton clothing is made of grows in Mississippi*.

When we first read this, we see *cotton clothing* as a single noun and expect to find out what it is made of. But when we reach *grows*, we have to go back and reinterpret the first half of the sentence. To avoid this, the sentence could be rewritten as *The cotton that clothing is made of grows in Mississippi*.

Other neat examples of garden path sentences are:

- The horse raced past the house fell.
- The old man the pumps.

- The prime number few.
- Fat people eat accumulates.

I'll leave you to work out how the sentences should be read.

This vacuum cleaner really sucks

While artificial languages such as computer languages are logical, real tongues refuse to follow the dictates of reason. Rules are there to be broken, but the defiance of logic in English is most noticeable when a single word or sentence can have two diametrically opposite meanings. When you say *This vacuum cleaner really sucks*, do you mean that it's effective or useless at cleaning? When you say *It's all downhill from here*, are you implying that things are going to get easier or worse?

There are a lot of potentially **self-contradictory sentences** in English. For instance, there are two possible continuations for each of the following sentences:

- They fought with the Greeks…
  …against the Romans.
  …and lost.
- I wasted no time doing it…
  …because it was important.
  …because I was too busy.
- Her intelligence is legendary…
  …and her reputation is well-deserved.
  …and she also wrongly believes she is beautiful.
- The alarm went off…
  …and we got up.
  …so we turned it back on.
- You can't be too proud of yourself…
  …after making so many mistakes.
  …with so many wonderful achievements.

It may seem that these sentences represent a special case, but English, as usual, has further peculiarities. There are quite a few words that can have two opposite meanings. These words are called **autoantonyms**, from *auto* meaning self (as in autobiography) and *antonym* meaning opposite.

The most commonly cited autoantonym is *cleave*. It can mean either stick tightly (e.g. The body glove will cleave to your body) or cut apart (e.g. A single blow can cleave a man). These two opposite meanings are simply a coincidence of history. The first comes from the Old English word *clifian*, while the second is derived from another Old English word, *cleofan*. As words change over time, purely by chance the two different Old English words have both come to be rendered as *cleave* in modern English.

Other autoantonyms come about for different reasons. Some may be due to a word adding new meanings to its original definition. For example, *fast* in Old English meant firmly fixed (a meaning retained in phrases such as *stand fast* and *hold fast*). While keeping this meaning, the word also took on new meanings. First, the firm aspect of the sense was extended to include *strong* and *vigorous*; then, this last aspect was again broadened to give the current meaning of fast as *quick*.

A third way in which autoantonyms are created occurs when words are used as different parts of speech, such as when a noun is employed as a verb. For instance, *screen* was originally a noun, but then people started to use it as a verb. Some used *screen* to mean project onto a screen, while others created the meaning of hide with a screen, which also took on a metaphorical sense. Because of these two extensions of a noun into a verb, a sentence such as *The censors screened the movie* could have two opposite intentions based on the opposite senses of screen.

Other autoantonyms in English are illustrated by the following pairs of sentences. *Bolt* can mean leave quickly or secure firmly:

- The horse bolted.
- I bolted the table to the floor.

Dust can mean remove dust or sprinkle with particles:

- I dusted the chair.
- I dusted the cake.

Impregnable can mean impossible to enter or able to be impregnated:

- The fortress is impregnable.
- She is impregnable.

Oversight can mean supervision or careless omission:

- Her oversight prevented the disaster.
- Her oversight caused the disaster.

Resign can mean quit or sign up again:

- He resigned from the job.
- He resigned for the job.

A seriously funny chapter

While English makes no attempt to be consistent, generally there are patterns and rules underlying the language, even if these patterns have more exceptions than examples following the rules. There are, however, some phrases that are strikingly incongruous, and these are called **oxymorons**. How can events be *seriously funny*? How can people be *awfully nice*? And how can we have *bad health*?

Oxymorons have a rich history. Shakespeare played with illogicalities in *A Midsummer Night's Dream*:

> 'A tedious brief scene of young Pyramus
> And his love Thisbe; very tragical mirth.'
> Merry and tragical! tedious and brief!
> That is, hot ice and wondrous strange snow.
> How shall we find the concord of this discord?

More recently, some suggested oxymorons smack more of social comment than a true lack of logic: *military intelligence, Microsoft Works* and *civil engineer*.

The true beauty of oxymorons is that, unless we sit back and really think, we happily accept them as normal, logical English. So many people would read the following passage without a second thought about its being riddled with inconsistencies.

> *It was an* open secret *that the company had used a* paid volunteer *to test the* plastic glasses. *Although they were made using* liquid gas *technology and were an* original copy *that looked* almost exactly *like a more expensive*

brand, the volunteer thought that they were pretty ugly and that it would be simply impossible for the general public to accept them. On hearing this feedback, the company board was clearly confused and there was a deafening silence. This was a minor crisis and the only choice was to drop the product line.

Redundancies in close proximity

A lot of the things we say are redundant. Often we include words that are simply not needed. When a newspaper article talks about an *anonymous stranger*, it's difficult to see why the word anonymous needs to be there. After all, if someone's a stranger you don't know their name, so by definition they're anonymous. Similarly, we may talk about things being in *close proximity*, but what other kind of proximity is possible? Can things be in distant proximity? These redundancies are technically termed **pleonasms**.

Many pleonasms (such as *advance forward, merge together, sink down, undergraduate student, completely annihilated, new discovery, absolutely essential, past experience, free gift* and *handwritten manuscript*) have become so widely used that we don't stop to reflect on their redundancy.

An even more noticeable form of **redundant language**, and one that is becoming more common, involves abbreviations. *HIV* stands for human immune-deficiency virus, and yet we often talk about the *HIV virus* or, in full, the human immune-deficiency virus virus. Even worse, we might talk about the *CNN news network* (or the Cable News Network news network) and an *ABS braking system* (or an Anti-lock Braking System braking system). These redundant abbreviations have become so common in the field of technology that we could easily imagine a single sentence containing six examples:

> *The original ATM machine requiring a PIN number was based on a PC computer running the DOS operating system with an AC current and LCD display.*

Such unintentional redundancies can trip up almost any speaker. We use the abbreviations without thinking about what they stand for. While we may use redundancies without worry every day, when someone in the public eye does so they are often pulled up for it. Some celebrities are renowned for their pleonastic **tautologies**. For instance:

- Calvin Coolidge (30th US President): 'When large numbers of men are unable to find work, unemployment results.'
- Brooke Shields (actress): 'Smoking can kill you, and if you've been killed, you've lost a very important part of your life.'
- Dan Quayle (44th US Vice President and the favourite of any author looking for examples of misuse of language): 'If we do not succeed, we run the risk of failure.'

Tautologies (or necessarily true statements) such as these can also lead to amusing aphorisms. Two of the best practitioners of the art of creating tautologous aphorisms are Samuel Goldwyn, the movie mogul, and Yogi Berra, the baseball player and manager.

From Samuel Goldwyn:

- 'Anyone who goes to a psychiatrist ought to have his head examined.'
- 'I never make predictions, especially about the future.'
- 'Go see the movie, and see for yourself why you shouldn't see it.'

From Yogi Berra:

∞ 'It's déjà vu all over again.'

∞ 'Sometimes you can observe a lot just by watching.'

∞ 'A nickel ain't worth a dime any more.'

There ain't never been no better chapter

Double negatives (and triple negatives such as the title of this chapter) are frowned on nowadays, but the disapproval of double negatives is fairly recent. Before the nineteenth century (and in many other languages such as Greek), double negatives were used for emphasis – a sentence with a double negative meant that the negative aspect was heavily stressed. Thus Chaucer wrote, *There wasn't no man nowhere so virtuous.*

Ignoring the fact that languages are not governed by mathematics, the Victorians, with their passion for logic, decided that two negatives cancelled each other out, so producing an affirmative. Thus a sentence like *Nobody didn't go* was said to have changed its meaning from 'nobody went' to 'everybody went'.

In spite of the general admonition to avoid double negatives, they were still sometimes used for emphasis. For example, in *Dombey and Son* by Charles Dickens, the butler says that he would *never hear of no foreigner never boning nothing out of no travelling chariot.* Trying to resolve so many successive negatives is a waste of time, as they are clearly meant to reinforce each other. More recently, double negatives have been used to indicate a certain lack of education in the speaker. Pink Floyd in 'The Wall' sang: *We don't need no education; we don't need no thought control.*

Trying to decide whether two negatives should be viewed as a positive or not can become even more confusing in poorly expressed writing. For example, take the sentence:

> He went quietly, but not so quietly that his going failed to escape the notice of the policeman.

Did the policeman notice his going or not? Similarly with the sentence:

I do not think it is possible that the two conflicting philosophies should fail to lead to separate parties.

Will there be two parties or not?

Another peculiar feature of negatives in English is that there are some negative words for which no positive equivalent exists. For example, if someone with a plain face is *nondescript*, shouldn't someone else whose face is never likely to be forgotten be called *descript*, meaning particularly memorable? If a well-behaved person has *impeccable* manners, does a brat have *peccable* manners? And if instead of seeing *neither hide nor hair* of a friend you do meet them, would you see *both hide and hair* of them?

The following paragraph contains several examples of negative words and phrases for which no positive equivalents exist.

I was feeling very chalant when I walked into her room. She was perfection – her hair was kempt, her clothes hevelled, her movements gainly, and her whole aspect gruntled. It would be skin off my nose if someone so perfect didn't like me. Beknownst to me, she preferred to know everything about a person before meeting them, so, after making bones about it with my companion, I had been travelling cognito.

Part VII

Language Play

Wit's the noblest frailty of the mind.

Thomas Shadwell

The range of uses of language is incredible. We can employ many of the same words to write an academic political polemic and to crack an asinine childish joke. In this part we look at the latter – the playful side of English.

Most language-based jokes are puns, of which the special type called a Tom Swifty is a particularly notable example. But not all amusing turns of language are intentional – there are the infamous Spoonerisms and malapropisms, which can lead to loud guffaws as well as red faces. And not all language play is intended to be funny – there's also the clever creation of palindromes.

A good pun is its own reword

Puns – plays on words – are generally viewed as the worst of jokes. They are met with groans rather than laughter, and people who regularly make puns are not well regarded. Lewis Carroll, the author of *Alice in Wonderland*, once wrote: 'The Good and Great must ever shun that reckless and abandoned one who stoops to perpetrate a pun', while British playwright John Dennis went one step further by imputing a lack of morals to the creator of a bad pun: 'A man who could make so vile a pun would not scruple to pick a pocket.'

Usually a pun involves either a single word with two meanings or two similar-sounding words. An example of the former, playing on two senses of the word *charge*, is:

> *The farmer lets people walk across the field for free, but the bull charges.*

For the latter type, the equivalent sounds of *cereal* and *serial* lead to the following pun:

> *At breakfast I am so hungry I can murder a bowl of muesli. Does that make me a cereal killer?*

Puns are funny (or groan inducing depending on your temperament) because they activate two possible interpretations in your brain. As writer Arthur Koestler put it: 'In the pun, two strings of thought are tangled into one acoustic knot.' Knowing why a pun is funny, however, reduces the level of humour – a constant problem for humourologists, whose analyses of jokes make the profession one with the fewest opportunities for amusement. So rather than analysing further, let's start making some puns.

The following sentences can be turned into puns by adding appropriate terms in the spaces. Can you think of suitable words?

>Condoms should be used on every .... occasion.
>A gossip is someone with a great sense of.........
>When you dream in colour, it's a .... of your imagination.
>Shotgun wedding: a case of .... or death.
>A hangover is the .... of ....
>A Freudian slip is when you say one thing but mean ....
>A bicycle can't stand by itself because it is ....
>Beauty is in the eye of the ....

Despite a general shunning of puns, there are some famous ones. My favourite is James Joyce's description of some girls as *jung and easily freudened*. But perhaps the best-known pun is the telegram sent by Sir Charles Napier after his forces captured the Indian province of Sind. The single word in the telegram was *Peccavi* – the Latin for 'I have sinned'. Unfortunately, as with many good stories, there was in fact no such telegram. The word Peccavi only appeared in a cartoon about the incident in the satirical magazine *Punch*.

While perhaps not as clever as these famous examples, I hope that those in the quiz still elicited a chuckle:

☞ Condoms should be used on every *conceivable* occasion.

- A gossip is someone with a great sense of *rumour*.
- When you dream in colour it's a *pigment* of your imagination.
- Shotgun wedding: a case of *wife* or death.
- A hangover is the *wrath* of *grapes*.
- A Freudian slip is when you say one thing but mean *your mother*.
- A bicycle can't stand by itself because it is *two tired*.
- Beauty is in the eye of the *beer holder*.

'We're out of whisky,' Tom said dispiritedly

The title of this chapter is an example of a special kind of pun called a **Tom Swifty**. The typical Tom Swifty consists of a quoted sentence followed by 'Tom said' and an adverb. The pun lies in the link between the quoted sentence and the subsequent adverb. A few other examples are:

- ❧ 'Can I get you something?' Tom asked fetchingly.
- ❧ 'Do you want to buy some salmon?' Tom asked selfishly.
- ❧ 'I manufacture tabletops for shops,' Tom said counterproductively.
- ❧ 'I forgot what I was supposed to buy,' Tom said listlessly.
- ❧ 'Venus de Milo is beautiful,' Tom said disarmingly (or even 'armlessly).

To see how creative you are at making Tom Swifties, try to add an appropriate adverb to the following sentences to make a pun.

'Who was Pope before John Paul I?' Tom asked......
'I have forgotten the German word for "four",' Tom said......
'Is that Timothy or Russell?' Tom asked......
'Thank you, Monsieur,' Tom said......
'...you lose some,' Tom said......
'I only get *Newsweek*,' Tom said......
'Who was Bill Clinton's vice president?' Tom asked......
'Elvis is dead,' Tom said......

There are other ways of making Tom Swifties. The next most common method is to use an appropriate reporting verb after the quoted sentence. For instance:

- ❧ 'That leprechaun isn't telling the truth,' Tom implied.
- ❧ 'My grape juice has fermented,' Tom whined.
- ❧ 'I need another layer of mulch on my garden,' Tom repeated.
- ❧ 'I want to renew my membership,' Tom rejoined.

Other more complex variations can be seen in the following examples:

- ❧ 'We like fairy tales,' said Tom's brothers grimly.
- ❧ 'Don't let me drown in Egypt,' said Tom, deep in denial.
- ❧ 'Don't add too much water,' said Tom with great concentration.
- ❧ 'I won't finish in fifth place,' Tom held forth.

The name Tom Swifty comes from a series of boys' adventure books written by Victor Appleton (a pseudonym for Edward L. Stratemeyer). In these books, nearly everything the hero Tom Swift said was qualified with a following adverb. Unfortunately these weren't puns, but they did lead to the pastiche now known as Tom Swifties.

To finish off with, here are my eight favourite Tom Swifties:

- ❧ 'Who was Pope before John Paul I?' Tom asked piously.
- ❧ 'I have forgotten the German word for "four",' Tom said fearlessly.
- ❧ 'Is that Timothy or Russell?' Tom asked timorously.

- 'Thank you, Monsieur,' Tom said mercifully.
- '...you lose some,' Tom said winsomely.
- 'I only get *Newsweek*,' Tom said timelessly.
- 'Who was Bill Clinton's vice president?' Tom asked allegorically.
- 'Elvis is dead,' Tom said expressly.

Tips of the slung

One special type of slip of the tongue is the **Spoonerism**, whereby letters or syllables get swapped around in a phrase. The Spoonerism is named after the Reverend William Archibald Spooner, an Oxford history professor who was famous for committing these slips. For example, instead of asking a secretary *Is the Dean busy?*, the professor accidentally swapped around the initial letters of the last two words to produce *Is the bean dizzy?* Other allegedly genuine examples from the Reverend Spooner include the following:

- To a student: *You have hissed my mystery lecture.*
- As a toast: *Three cheers for our queer old dean.*
- In church: *The Lord is thy shoving leopard.*
- Quoting *I Corinthians* 13:12: *For now we see through a dark, glassly.*
- Officiating at a wedding: *It is now kisstomary to cuss the bride.*
- To another student: *You have tasted two worms.*
- At a naval review: *This vast display of cattle ships and bruisers.*
- To a meeting of farmers: *I see before me tons of soil.*
- To a stranger in church: *I believe you are occupewing my pie. May I sew you to another sheet?*

In addition to slips of the tongue, Spooner was also famed for his absent-mindedness. He once invited a fellow lecturer to a tea 'to welcome our new archaeology Fellow'. The lecturer protested, 'But sir, I am our new archaeology Fellow.' Spooner replied, 'Never mind. Come all the same.'

Here are a few more Spoonerisms. What was originally intended?

> At the lead of spite.
> Go and shake a tower.
> It's roaring with pain.
> Wearing a cat flap.
> Dealt a blushing crow.

While the above examples simply lead to mirth (and possibly embarrassment for the speaker), several phrases in English lend themselves to naughty, and in some cases obscene, Spoonerisms:

- She showed me her tool kits.
- He's a smart fella.
- It's the Tale of Two Cities.
- You really are a shining wit.
- The acrobats displayed some cunning stunts.
- He's not a pheasant plucker.

The last of these is the root of the tongue-twisting verse:

> I'm not a pheasant plucker,
> I'm a pheasant plucker's mate.
> I'm only plucking pheasants
> 'Cos the pheasant plucker's late.

Similarly, Spoonerisms are the root of various schoolboy jokes, such as:

> What's the difference between a bad archer and a constipated owl?
> One can shoot but can't hit, and the other...

The less said about these naughty Spoonerisms the better. To end more cleanly, there is also a neat Spooneristic aphorism:

It's better to have a bottle in front of me than a frontal lobotomy.

The use of the oracular tongue

In an attempt to gain long-lasting renown, it may be worth acquiring a habitual but strange linguistic tic. If peculiar enough, the tic could lead to the fame derived from having a figure of speech named after you. In the last chapter we saw how the Reverend Spooner became widely known, and in this chapter we will examine the legacy of Mrs Malaprop: the **malapropism**.

Mrs Malaprop, unfortunately, was not a real person. Rather, she was a character in *The Rivals*, a 1775 comedy by Richard Sheridan. In the play, Mrs Malaprop was accused of using uncommon words that she didn't really understand. Her reply was: 'Sure, if I *reprehend* anything in this world, it is the use of my *oracular* tongue and a nice *derangement* of *epitaphs*' (when she wanted to use *apprehend*, *vernacular*, *arrangement* and *epithets*). A malapropism, then, is the comic, and usually unintentional, use of an inappropriate word.

In writing, malapropisms are normally the result of confusion between similar-sounding words:

- He's a wolf in *cheap* clothing.
- The girl was wearing a beautiful *pendulum* round her neck.
- I received an email *portending* to be from the unfortunate son of the late President.
- Her *insinuendo* was totally unwarranted.

These are rarely very amusing. However, a good source of humorous written malapropisms is students' essays. Here's a selection of my favourites:

- For drowning, climb on top of the person and move up and down to make artificial perspiration.
- The Bible is full of interesting caricatures.
- Columbus was a great navigator who discovered America while cursing about the Atlantic.
- David was a Hebrew king skilled at playing the liar.
- The correct way to find the key to a piece of music is to use a pitchfork.
- Music sung by two people at the same time is called a duel; if they sing without music it is called Acapulco.
- The principal singer of nineteenth-century opera was called pre-Madonna.
- If you are buying a house, a mortgage company will insist you are well endowed.
- Louis Pasteur discovered a cure for rabbis.
- Socrates died from an overdose of wedlock.
- The equator is a menagerie lion running around the Earth through Africa.

In addition to malapropisms, students' essays often contain humorous illogicalities derived from misplacing parts of sentences. Here are my favourites:

- Abraham Lincoln wrote the Gettysburg Address while traveling from Washington to Gettysburg on the back of an envelope.
- Another tale tells of William Tell, who shot an arrow through an apple while standing on his son's head.

Truly amusing written malapropisms are rare. There are, however, plenty of pairs of **easily confused words** in English that can trip up even the most literate. What's the difference between *biannual* and *biennial*, *flout* and *flaunt*, and *imply* and *infer*? Should it be *continual* or *continuous*, *principle* or *principal*, *venal* or *venial*?

The etymologies of some of these pairs are worth quickly following up for interest. Strangely, *flout* comes from the Middle English word *flowten*, meaning to play a flute. This shifted sense to *jeer* before taking on its current meaning. *Flaunt*, on the other hand, is probably related to *vaunt*, as in his much-vaunted ability. And for another pair, *venal*, meaning for sale (think of a venal politician), has the same root as *vendor*. In contrast, *venial* derives ultimately from *venus* meaning sexual love, coming by way of a shift in sense to forgiveness in order to take on its current meaning of pardonable. Although a frequent source of malapropisms, misusing pairs of easily confused words is more of an annoyance than an amusement.

In spoken language, on the other hand, malapropisms abound as the mouth can move faster than the brain. Two of the worst offenders are politicians and sports commentators. Typical of the former is George W. Bush, whose malapropisms include:

- The law I sign today directs new funds ... to the task of collecting vital intelligence ... on weapons of mass production.
- It will take time to restore chaos and order.
- I am mindful not only of preserving executive powers for myself, but for predecessors as well.

The malapropisms and other mistakes made by sports commentators occur so frequently that there is a special word specifically for them: **Colemanballs** (after the British sports commentator David Coleman). Here are a few typical Colemanballs.

- ೦౦ This boy swims like a greyhound.
- ೦౦ Tahamata went through the air like a torpedo.
- ೦౦ This series has been swings and pendulums all the way through.
- ೦౦ It's a unique occasion – a repeat of Melbourne 1977.
- ೦౦ It's especially tense for Parker who's literally fighting for a place on an overcrowded plane to India.
- ೦౦ And England win by a solitary nine runs.
- ೦౦ For a player to ask for a transfer has opened everybody's eyebrows.
- ೦౦ And Keegan was there like a surgeon's knife – bang!

Many of the most amusing Colemanballs are not true malapropisms. Rather, they involve illogicalities.

My favourite is:

Some of the players never dreamed they'd be playing in a Cup Final at Wembley – but here they are today, fulfilling those dreams.

While malapropisms are inappropriate things that we say or write, there is also a variant based on what we hear. Instead of the speaker or writer making a mistake, in the case of **mondegreens** it is the listener who misunderstands what is heard. A mondegreen involves mishearing the lyrics of a song, and is named after the supposed Lady Mondegreen in the song 'The Bonny Earl of Murray' (which in fact contains the lyrics 'And laid him on the green').

Below are the four most commonly cited mondegreens, all from well-known pop songs. Do you know the correct version?

> The ants are my friends.
> Scuse me while I kiss this guy.
> There's a bathroom on the right.
> The girl with colitis goes by.

Since I live in Thailand, the most meaningful mondegreen for me was my own mishearing of a line from The Jam's 'Eton Rifles'. Instead of the correct 'What chance do you have against a tie and a crest?', for years I heard 'What chance do you have against a Thai in a dress?'. There's always a chance of mishearing lyrics such as:

- ∞ 'The answer, my friends' – from 'Blowin' in the Wind', by Bob Dylan.
- ∞ 'Scuse me while I kiss the sky' – from 'Purple Haze' by Jimi Hendrix.
- ∞ 'There's a bad moon on the rise' – from 'Bad Moon Rising' by Creedence Clearwater Revival.
- ∞ 'The girl with kaleidoscope eyes' – from 'Lucy in the Sky with Diamonds' by The Beatles.

Of course, with the unclear enunciation in many pop songs, it's likely that new mondegreens will carry on being created.

Ailihphilia

One of the strangest features of language concerns **palindromes**. A palindrome is a word or sentence that reads the same back to front. So a word such as *eye* is a palindrome, in that if you start with the last letter and work backwards, the new reading is still eye. And it's not only short words that are palindromic. A few longer words, such as *redivider*, are also palindromes.

Most palindromes exist simply by happenchance — there's no specific reason for *eye*, for instance, to be a palindrome, it just is. For the longer words, the existence of pairs of prefixes and suffixes such as the *re-* and *-er* in redivider increases the likelihood of palindromic words.

Can you think of palindromic words with the following meanings?
> Something that spins
> Decorate again
> Canoe
> Fast competitive vehicle
> Method of detecting aircraft

More interesting than palindromic words, such as *rotor*, *repaper*, *kayak*, *racecar* and *radar*, are palindromic sentences. The most famous is *A man, a plan, a canal — Panama*, first recorded in 1948. Again, starting with the last letter and reading backwards results in the same sentence as a normal reading. Palindromic sentences have been around for a long time, with both the ancient Greeks and Romans using them. For example, the Romans had a riddle that went:

In girum imus nocte et consumimur igni

meaning 'We enter the circle at night and are consumed by fire' (the answer to the riddle is a moth).

Once you know the first half of a palindrome, it's fairly straightforward to complete the whole sentence. For example, if you're aware that a palindrome starts *Do geese...*, reading backwards we find *see God*. So the whole palindrome is *Do geese see God?* Other nice examples of palindromic sentences include:

- Some men interpret nine memos.
- Never odd or even.
- Are we not drawn onward, we few, drawn onward to a new era.
- Dogma: I am God.

By inserting palindromic sentences into the middle of other palindromic sentences, long palindromes can be created. For example, *Madam, I'm Adam* can be expanded to *Madam, in Eden I'm Adam*. The longest palindrome is probably a 4,963-word monster that starts:

> *Star? Not I! Movie – it too has a star in or a cameo who wore mask – cast are livewires*

You can work out for yourself how this palindrome ends.

Normal sentence structure is at a premium in constructing palindromes. It's much easier to make contrived palindromes than ones that read like natural English. Allowing for such inelegant constructions, palindromes have been designed starting (and of course ending) with 25 of the letters of the alphabet – with the exception of *q*, which is normally only found in combination with *u* at the start of words.

A couple of interesting variations are **word-unit palindromes** and **palindromic squares**.

A word-unit palindrome is one that, at the word level, forms the same sentence when read backwards. Word-unit palindromes make nice aphorisms, such as:

Women understand men; few men understand women.

A palindromic square contains words that can be read in either direction in every row and column. For example:

N	E	T		S	T	E	P
E	W	E		T	I	M	E
T	E	N		E	M	I	T
				P	E	T	S

The largest palindromic square created in English is a 6×6 square, but examples of these include very obscure words like *esssse*, which as we saw in the chapter on double letters means ashes.

If you're interested in creating your own palindromes, here are a few helpful pointers:

- ∾ The letter *h* can cause a lot of problems and is best avoided.
- ∾ Make a list of words that can be read backwards as other words, for instance *rats* and *star*, *live* and *evil*, *on* and *no*. These can then be combined to form a sentence: *Rats live on no evil star*. There are even useful

pairs of words for less usual letters such as *jar* and *raj*, and *Zeus* and *Suez*.

∞   Don't start your palindromic sentence with the letter *q* – no one has ever managed to come up with an example.

∞   To create a word square with an odd number of letters, the middle row (and column) must be a palindromic word.

Have fun!

A miscellany of curiosities

W hile the rest of the book has explored many of the most bizarre aspects of the language, there is a massive range of other odd features still left unexamined. For example, there are the common English words, notorious to poets, which don't have rhymes. Most infamous of these unrhymable words is *orange* (which only has half-rhymes, such as lozenge). Others include *chimney*, *depth*, *pint* and *purple*.

Along similar lines are the words ending in letter combinations that you would think would be common but are in fact restricted to one or two words only. The best known of these rare word-ending letter combinations is -*gry*, made famous by an annoying riddle that has made its way around the internet several times: 'There are three words in English which end in -gry. Angry is one, hungry is another. What is the third word?' Excluding obscure words, there are no other words in English ending in -*gry* – the riddle is a trick. Other surprisingly rare word endings in English include -*nen*, found in *linen*, -*ln* found in *kiln* and *Lincoln*, and -*igy* found in *prodigy* and *effigy*.

Also unusual are typewriter words, which can be typed using only certain parts of the Qwertyuiop keyboard (so well known that British author Anthony Burgess named the main character of one of his novels *Qwert Yuiop*). *Typewriter* itself only uses letters from the top row. For the record, the longest word that can be typed using only the top row is *rupturewort*, a herbal shrub, while *alfalfas*, another plant, is the longest word possible from the middle row. Unfortunately, the lack of vowels on the bottom row precludes its sole use to type words.

If you type professionally using all ten fingers (unlike my own clumsy two-fingered attempts), you can type *stewardesses* using only your left hand and *polyphony* with only your right. Using alternating hands, the longest word possible is *dismantlement*.

Another type of keyboard is the piano keyboard, which allows the creation of musical words. The notes on this keyboard go from *A* to *G*, which allows a word like *baggage* to be played as music. Indeed, the nineteenth-century Irish composer John Field actually wrote a melody to thank some dinner hosts for a wonderful meal. The tune includes the sequences *B-E-E-F* and *C-A-B-B-A-G-E*.

English is such a fascinating language that it can enliven academic subjects traditionally seen as dry, like maths, biology and chemistry. In chemistry, a surprisingly high number of elements are named after places. There include *americium*, *californium*, *europium*, *francium* and *germanium*. The place that has provided the most inspiration for naming chemicals is a rare-mineral quarry near Ytterby in Sweden, after which are named the elements *erbium*, *terbium*, *ytterbium* and *yttrium*.

However, it's the more complex chemicals that provide the fun. The mineral magnesium iron silicate hydroxide was first found near the town of Cummington in Massachusetts. Using the place as the inspiration, the mineral was named *cummingtonite*. Similarly, the mineral *burpalite* is named after the Burpala massif in Russia where it can be found. Then there's a ring-shaped chemical called *arsole*, a poisonous molecule called *vomicine*, and a plant-derived chemical called *megaphone*.

Chemistry is also a good source of acronyms. Aryl selenide, a poisonous and smelly chemical, is usually referred to in the shorthand version *ArSe*; diethyl azodicarboxylate, a carcinogen, is shortened to *DEAD*; sodium ethyl xanthate is *SEX*; and the toxic diaminomaleonitrile is more commonly known as *DAMN*.

In biology, probably the greatest source of amusing terms is genetics. Every time a new gene is identified, it needs to be named. So a gene that makes insects grow spines was named *hedgehog*, and variants on it have the names *sonic hedgehog*, *desert hedgehog* and even *tiggy-winkle hedgehog*. More recently, and at a particularly apposite time, a gene controlling puberty was discovered and named *Harry Potter*.

Even mathematics becomes intriguing when viewed from a linguistic perspective. For instance, *four* is the only number where the number of letters equals the numeral itself. *Forty* is the only number with its letters in alphabetical order, while *one* is the only number using reverse alphabetical order. Similarly, *first* is the only ordinal number (first, second, third etc.) with its letters in alphabetical order.

English is also a bestial language. People can be described as *top dogs*, *jackasses*, *parasites*, *stool pigeons* and *black sheep*, among a whole range of other animals whose characteristics are apparently applicable to humans. Similarly, people may *weasel* or *worm* their way into your affections by *crowing* about their achievements, *parroting* others' words or *ratting* out rivals. When dining, they may *eat like a horse* by *pigging out* and *wolfing the food down*. The sheer quantity of phrases with animal origins is enough to make you *clam up*.

I could go on and on exploring the bizarre byways of English, but I hope that, with all the examples in this book, I have shown why there has been, is and always will be *Much Ado about English*.

Sources

Books

Ayto, John (1993) *Dictionary of Difficult Words*, Helicon.

Bragg, Melvyn (2003) *The Adventure of English*, Sceptre.

Burgess, Anthony (1992) *A Mouthful of Air*, Vintage.

Fowler, H.W. (1965) *Fowler's Modern English Usage* (2nd edition revised by Sir Ernest Gowers), Oxford University Press.

Jack, Albert (2004) *Red Herrings and White Elephants*, Metro.

Lederer, Richard (1987) *Anguished English*, Pocket Books.

Lederer, Richard (1990) *The Play of Words*, Pocket Books.

Quinion, Michael (2004) *Port Out, Starboard Home and other Language Myths*, Penguin.

Soames, Catherine & Stevenson, Angus (eds) (2004) *Concise Oxford English Dictionary*, Oxford University Press.

Websites

Online Etymology Dictionary, http://www.etymonline.com

The Wordplay Website, http://www.fun-with-words.com

Wikipedia, http://www.wikipedia.org

Index